FAVORITE
CHILDREN
OF THE BIBLE

10 Sermons On The Lives
Of Children Of Scripture

BY R. BLAINE DETRICK

C.S.S. Publishing Co., Inc.
Lima, Ohio

___93 by
The C.S.S. Publishing Company, Inc.
Lima, Ohio

Library of Congress Cataloging-in-Publication Data

Detrick, R. Blaine, 1918-
    Favorite children of the Bible : 10 sermons on the lives of familiar children of scripture / by R. Blaine Detrick.
        121 p.   14 by 21.5 cm.
    ISBN 1-55673-511-1
    1. Children in the Bible — Sermons. 2. Sermons, American. I. Title.
BS576.D48   1993
220.9'2'083—dc20   92-35096
                                                                                                        CIP

9303 / ISBN 1-55673-511-1   PRINTED IN U.S.A.

To my "Favorite Children"

who "stand fast in the faith"
(1 Corinthians 10:13)

who "honor (their) father and mother"
(Ephesians 6:1)

to my children, Brian and Cheryl,

this book is tenderly dedicated.

"I thank my God upon every remembrance of you"
(Philippians 1:3)

"I have no greater joy than to hear that
my children walk in truth"
(3 John 4)

Table Of Contents

Introduction

One of the most rewarding and fruitful projects of my ministry was to have the congregation vote for its *Favorite Men Of The Bible* ... preach a series of sermons about the results ... and then write a book based on the experience.

It then, of course, was natural to follow the same pattern for the *Favorite Women Of The Bible* — which was done. And the women proved to be even more popular than the men!

The logical step, at that point, seemed to be to continue with the *Favorite Children Of The Bible.* The opportunity presented itself during the summer months, when our morning worship and our church school were merged into one family service. It was a successful effort — for both children and adults ... for both attendance and interest.

During the opening part of the sermon period, I simply tried to retell the Bible story — for the children. Then I sought to emphasize briefly some lessons — for the adults.

In these chapters, I have followed the same pattern. The interesting result was that many adults made it a point to tell me that they enjoyed the first part of the sermon more than the latter! This is not surprising, however, because the stories of the Bible are stimulating stories — whether about men, women or children. Each story carries its own message — and it speaks to everybody. What it says to you may not be the same as what it says to your neighbor or your friend. This is one advantage of biographical preaching — and this is one way in which the Holy Spirit does its work.

In this book, the "Favorite Children" were not selected by any kind of a ballot; I simply chose some of my own favorites.

They are presented here in chronological order — primarily because that's the method I used with "Favorite Men" and "Favorite Women."

Also to conform with my treatment of the men and the women, a Q-Sheet (originally an insert with the worship bulletin) is placed at the beginning of every chapter. Each Q-Sheet contains a quiz about the child whose story is told in that chapter and some questions to guide your personal thinking or a group discussion. These Q-Sheets may be reproduced for local use.

My recommendation is that you first give yourself the quiz without using a Bible! Then do use a Bible — to verify each answer. The correct answers are not listed anywhere — you will need to look up the biblical references to find them! My ultimate purpose, you see, is not only to have you read this book, but to have you read THE Book. And be sure to remember the purpose for which the holy scriptures were written — you'll find it in John 20:31.

After the quiz, your reading of the chapter should be more worthwhile and meaningful. Use the Q-Sheets ... use these chapters ... use the Bible.

Your reading may be done individually, in the privacy of your own home or your own heart. Or it may be done in groups: Bible study sessions ... youth groups ... study classes ... circle programs ... mid-week services and so on. This book could then serve as a workbook and be augmented by a discussion of the questions on the Q-Sheet.

The opening portion of each chapter (the retelling of the biblical story) can serve as the basic material for a children's Sunday school class — or might be read (or told) to any group of children.

Pastors may find the book useful for sermon ideas. If so, I would strongly urge them to provide copies of the Q-Sheet for the congregation. I have been amazed at the interest they created, the comments they stimulated, the discussion they generated.

All the quotations from the Bible, in this book, unless otherwise noted, are from the Authorized King James Version. I grew up with this version; I have been familiar with it; and I have done much memorizing from it. I enjoy and encourage the many modern translations; indeed, I use them constantly for study — but when it comes to quoting, I instinctively return to the King James Version.

I want to publicly acknowledge my gratitude to Mrs. Naomi Maurer for her many hours of assistance, and above all, to my incomparable wife, Marguerite, for her many years of patience and forbearance.

My prayer is this — that your perusal of these pages may be just half as profitable for you as the preparation has been for me.

R. Blaine Detrick

Part I — Some Old Testament Children

A
Secret
Babysitter

For personal reading:
Exodus 1:1—2:10; 15:20; Numbers 26:59

For public reading:
Exodus 2:1-10

Outline

The Bible Story

The Miraculous Providence Of God

The Effective Work Of God's Servants

Q-SHEET

A Secret Babysitter
Exodus 1:22—2:10; 7:7; 15:20
Numbers 26:59

Quiz: *(Fill in the blanks. Try first without a Bible; then use the verses to verify each answer.)*

1. Miriam's father was of the tribe of _____ (Exodus 2:1).

2. Miriam's mother was of the tribe of _____ (Exodus 2:1).

3. Miriam's father was named _____ (Numbers 26:59).

4. Miriam's mother was named _____ (Numbers 26:59).

5-7. Miriam had two brothers; the older, named _____, was _____ years older then the younger, named _____ (Numbers 26:59; Exodus 7:7).

8, 9. _____ ordered that all Jewish boy babies were to be _____ (Exodus 1:22).

10-12. Miriam's baby brother was _____ months old when his mother used _____ to prepare an _____ for him (Exodus 2:2, 3).

11

13-15. Miriam's baby brother was discovered by the daughter

of _____ when she came, with her

_____, to the river to _____
(Exodus 2:5).

16. Miriam's baby brother _____ when he was found (Exodus 2:6).

17. Miriam brought her own mother to be a _____ for the baby (Exodus 2:7-9).

18. Miriam grew up and became a _____ (Exodus 15:20).

Questions: *(for individual consideration and/or group discussion)*

1. Why has anti-Semitism (hatred of Jews) been so continual for centuries? What can we do about it (Exodus 1:7-14)?

2. How does Pharaoh's effort at population control compare with ready access to abortion (Exodus 1:22)?

3. What should be our attitude toward the ordination and acceptance of women pastors (Exodus 15:20)?

4. Did it "just happen" that the princess went to the river at precisely the right time — or does the hand of the Lord help to create such a coincidence? Tell of an illustration from your own experience (Exodus 2:3-6).

A Secret Babysitter

Allow me, for a few moments, to write for the boys and girls, although the rest of you may read along, if you wish.

Have you ever expected a baby brother or a baby sister? Perhaps Mother and Dad had told you that a new brother or sister would soon be coming into your home — and you were excited. At a time like that, you sort of wonder — about a lot of things.

The little girl that we are thinking about was expecting a brother or a sister. By the way, her name isn't even mentioned in the Bible story — she is simply called the "sister." Do you know her name? That's right — it was Miriam.

Miriam was expecting a brother or a sister. We don't know whether she had any preference. She already had one brother — his name was Aaron, and he was about three years old (Exodus 7:7). We don't know whether she wanted another brother, or a sister. The Bible doesn't say.

We do know, though, that she was living in a slave family. Miriam was a Hebrew — and the Egyptians had made the Hebrews their slaves. The Egyptians forced the Hebrews to work hard — so hard that some of them just couldn't stand it — they became sick, and died. But, overall, instead of getting weaker, the Hebrews were getting stronger — and more numerous. Their masters were afraid. The Egyptians said, "The Hebrews are becoming too powerful; we must do something."

Finally, the king (Pharaoh was another name for him) commanded, "All newborn Hebrew boy babies must be thrown into the river and drowned." For this reason, I wonder if Miriam didn't prefer a sister rather than a brother. I would think so. But when the baby was born, it was a boy — Miriam had another brother.

Now, the mother and father loved their new baby. They didn't want to destroy him, so they tried to hide him.

For the first three months of the life of her new brother, can't you imagine Miriam learning to watch over him . . . shush him . . . keep him quiet? Especially if there were soldiers passing the home — at any time of day or night. I'm sure that was a part of Miriam's life.

Babies don't make much noise — most of the time. When they do make noise, they make plenty of it. But much of the time — when they're newly born — they sleep.

Finally, though, after three months of constant vigilance . . . dangerous tension . . . and narrow escapes, the mother and father realized that there was no way to hide their baby any longer. The soldiers were certain to find him. And when the soldiers found him, they would take him down to the river . . . throw him in . . . and drown him.

These parents trusted God. And they believed that their baby was very special. So the mother took some bulrushes — the high reeds from along the river bank — and began to weave them. She wove them into a little basket . . . a little boat, a little ark. Then she took — mud! And she daubed it on the boat — to keep out the water, so it wouldn't leak.

Then she found some soft cloth, lined the bottom of the basket with it, and placed her baby in the little ark.

The mother then went down to the edge of the river and left the ark there — concealed among the reeds. And she told Miriam, "Watch over him . . . stay here . . . keep yourself hidden . . . and see what happens."

Now I don't know whether Miriam was scared. How would you have felt if you had been there? I'm sure that some of you have been babysitters for smaller children. But that was her baby brother, in the tiny boat, floating in the river. Would you have been frightened?

While she was watching (we don't know how long she was there), she heard some voices. "Somebody is coming," she whispered to herself. She peeked out of the bulrushes . . . looked around . . . and, sure enough, saw a group of women. They were coming down to the river — to go swimming, to bathe.

And when she looked closely, Miriam could tell from the design on her dress that one of the women was the princess — the daughter of the Pharaoh. I can just imagine Miriam's heart going pit-a-pat, pit-a-pat. "What is she going to do? ... What am I going to do? ... What's going to happen?" she thought to herself.

The women went down to the bank of the river — right near the very place where the little ark was floating. They were washing, when — suddenly, they heard an unexpected noise. "That sounds like a baby," exclaimed one of them.

As they searched the area, one of them pointed and said, "Look, there's a strange little basket out there — in the bulrushes."

The princess spoke to one of her maids, "Go, and bring it to me." (All this time, Miriam was off to one side, watching.)

The maid went out, picked up the little boat, and brought it back. The princess looked in the ark, and with a startled expression, said, "Why, it's a Hebrew baby!"

And just at that moment, Moses (that was the baby's name) started to cry. The princess reached down into the little boat ... took out the baby ... cuddled him ... patted him on the back ... cradled him in her arms and rocked him gently. He stopped crying. (The Bible doesn't say all of this, but I imagine it happened something like this.)

We all know how lovable babies can be. I imagine that just then, Moses became that cute. Anyhow, the princess seemed to fall in love with the baby she had discovered.

Miriam was watching all of this — from her hiding place in the reeds. Now she knew that she didn't have to worry about this princess. She realized that the princess wasn't as cruel as her father. And she was certain that she didn't need to be anxious about her baby brother now.

So she ventured out, and bowed before the princess. She did not say, "I am the baby's sister."

But she did volunteer, "Would you like me to go and find a nurse from among the Hebrew women — to take care of the baby for you?"

15

And the princess spoke that one important word — actually, the whole life of a nation depended on it — "Go."

The princess must have known what her father would have done — he would have had the baby killed immediately. But she fell in love with the baby — and preserved his life.

I think that secret babysitter had much wisdom and a great deal of courage to do what she did. Put yourself in her situation and consider: What would you have done if you had been watching over a baby along the river's bank, and a princess came and found it?

The Miraculous Providence of God

This story tells us many truths that we need to remember today. Let me mention two of them.

First of all, this story teaches us about the miraculous providence of God. When I use words like these, it doesn't seem as if I am thinking about children, does it? And yet I am, too. We all need to know what God's providence means.

God spared the life of the baby, named Moses, because he had a great purpose for that baby to accomplish. God was watching over all of these events. Interestingly enough — see how the providence of God works — Moses was spared from death by the very river (the Nile River) that was supposed to destroy him! And he was saved by the daughter of the very king who had decreed that he should die! Isn't it amazing — how God controls life! And how a babysitter helped him!

Remember too how, a long time later, there was another baby boy who was spared, when another wicked king ordered that babies should die — around Bethlehem. But God had spoken to Mary and Joseph — and the baby Jesus had been carried away into a distant country (Matthew 2:13-16)! God overrules the wickedness of men. There is a familiar hymn by William Cowper that expresses this truth:

> "God moves in a mysterious way
> His wonders to perform."

The Effective Work Of God's Servants

The second idea that I emphasize from this story is the effective work of God's servants, those who love him ... trust him ... follow him ... obey him ... serve him.

Miriam was a little girl. Her name is not even mentioned in this part of the Bible. It is mentioned later on (Numbers 26:59), and we assume that this is the same sister. She just served God, doing what she was supposed to do ... very quietly ... unobtrusively ... without fanfare ... keeping in the background. Yet she helped God preserve the life of her baby brother, Moses, who grew up to be the great leader who molded the Hebrew people into a nation ... the great liberator who brought them into freedom and into the promised land ... the great law-giver who ascended the mountain and received the 10 commandments from the fingers of the Almighty God himself.

Had Miriam not been faithful, we don't know what might have happened. God would have needed to find some other way — perhaps some other person.

It is true of many girls, of many women: that they remain in the background ... that their names aren't well-known ... and yet they serve effectively and efficiently. Behind the outstanding male leaders, there is almost invariably some woman — a mother, a wife, a sister, a daughter — someone who cares, someone who loves.

Consider Moses. Think of the mother he had. Can you name her? (See Exodus 6:20; Numbers 26:59.) What a fine woman she must have been. What a wise, dedicated woman she must have been. What extraordinary hope and ingenuity she demonstrated: taking her baby ... placing him in a little ark by the edge of the river ... and trusting God for what would happen. Without her, Moses would never have been what he was.

Abraham had Sarah ... Jacob had Rachel ... Samuel had Hannah ... John Wesley had his mother, Susannah ... Abraham Lincoln had his mother, Nancy Hanks Lincoln. The well-known saying — that behind every famous man there stands a woman — is so true. (Someone has adjusted the familiar statement in this way: Behind every successful man, there stands an amazed mother-in-law!)

As a matter of fact, Miriam became a great woman on her own. Later, in the story of her life, she is called a prophetess (Exodus 15:20). Not very many women in the Bible days were called "prophetess." The Bible talks of many prophets, but few prophetesses (see Judges 4:4; 2 Kings 22:14, Nehemiah 6:14; Luke 2:36; Acts 21:9). Miriam is called a prophetess (she deserves a place in history for her own abilities) and eventually she is listed by name alongside her famous brothers, Moses and Aaron (Numbers 26:59; Micah 6:4).

Miriam, later on, did stumble and falter a bit (Numbers 12). She became envious and jealous, and had some difficulty because of this. I would like to forget that part of the story — but the Bible tells the whole truth about its people. She was forgiven; she was restored. But the key point is that Miriam was an authentic person, a child of God in her own right — not simply an extension of the men in her life.

What is true of women is also true of men. Many men serve God faithfully, in a dedicated way, but their names never make the front page — nor even the back page. They are humble, ordinary, everyday, obedient servants of God, content to remain out of the spotlight.

Great leaders would get nowhere without such followers. How many of the biblical leaders ... the historical leaders ... the military leaders ... our national leaders ... would be unknown had it not been for the people who were with them — their helpers, their followers, their assistants, their lieutenants?

For instance, you know about the great prophet, Jeremiah. But do you know about Baruch? We would not have heard about Jeremiah, except for Baruch. He was the scribe who took down Jeremiah's words (Jeremiah 36:4) and recorded them in a manuscript.

And when Baruch's scroll was written, an evil king took it ... slashed it with a pen-knife ... and tossed it into the flames of a nearby fireplace (Jeremiah 36:22, 23). But thank God for an almost unknown man, who saw to it that the priceless words of Jeremiah were written ... re-written ... and preserved (Jeremiah 36:32).

Did you ever hear of a man named Barnabas? Probably, but few of us realize what a debt we owe him. We might never have heard of Paul, the great apostle, if it hadn't been for Barnabas. When Paul (who was called Saul of Tarsus at that time) was converted on the road to Damascus, and finally returned to Jerusalem, the followers of Jesus had nothing to do with him. They reasoned, "There is no way we will trust that kind of a man. He has arrested the believers ... imprisoned them ... tortured them ... murdered them. We cannot believe that such a man could be changed."

It was Barnabas who met with Saul ... who believed him ... who trusted him and who put his arm around Saul's shoulders, and said, "I believe that God can transform any person, and I believe that God has changed this man." It was Barnabas who welcomed the new Saul into the fellowship of believers (Acts 9:26, 27).

Later on, Saul still got so much flak that he went back home — to Tarsus. Meantime, Barnabas continued to witness and serve. From Jerusalem, the apostles sent him — as a trouble-shooter — to the church at Antioch. This was the first city where gentiles (non-Jews) became believers and came into the church. It was also the place where believers were first called "Christians." Barnabas went to Antioch, was impressed, became a leader in the church and directed its growth and expansion.

At length, he said, "I know the man I need." So he himself journeyed over to Tarsus, found Saul, brought him to Antioch and put him to work in the Christian church (Acts 11:19-26).

Before long, Barnabas faded into near-obscurity. But had it not been for him, we might never have had the letters of Paul ... the journeys of Paul ... the teachings of Paul ... the achievements of Paul.

Think of other great persons who depended upon almost-unknown people. Did you ever hear of Eliezer? Abraham could not have done without him.

Ever hear of Joab ... or of Abishai ... or of Benaiah? Except for them, David never would have accomplished what he did.

Jesus had his friends — many of them unknown. He had 12 close disciples. Can you name them? Try it — see how many names you can write down. But whether or not we can name them, Jesus needed and depended upon those 12.

Paul, too, had many helpers. We quickly recall assistants like Barnabas ... Timothy ... Titus ... and Luke. But how about some of these: Tychicus ... Epaphras ... Epaphroditus ... Onesiphorus ... Lydia ... Priscilla? Ever hear of these people? Paul couldn't have done his work without them.

All leaders need devoted followers — a supporting cast of little-known persons. Every day, wherever we are — God wants us to serve him. Our true purpose is to obey and follow the Lord.

The first question of the ancient catechism was: "What is man's chief end?"

And the answer was, "Man's chief end is to glorify God and love him forever."

Our chief end is to glorify God. Sometimes we do this by being in the forefront; most times, we aren't. Sometimes we do this by standing in a pulpit, speaking to hundreds of people — but the service a preacher renders is no better than the service you can render — only different.

Uncle Billy was an elderly shut-in. One day, his pastor — a young man, still a seminary student — visited him.

When the pastor rose to leave, Uncle Billy said, "Pastor, would you read me a chapter from the Bible?"

"Why, certainly, I'd be glad to. Do you have any choice?"

"Yes, I do. I'd like for you to read a chapter, back in the book of Chronicles, where it has those long lists of the tribe of Judah, and the tribe of Levi, and the tribe of somebody else. I'd like you to read one of those long lists of strange names."

"Of course . . . I'll do that . . . but tell me why. Why would you want something like that? Wouldn't you prefer something closer to life, something helpful in meeting problems?"

"Well," replied Uncle Billy, "I'm not sure how you feel, but I have two reasons. In the first place, I've struggled over those names a lot of times, and I'd just like to hear somebody that can read them easily and pronounce them right. And the second thing is: there's a heap of comfort in those names for me. Here are lots of people. Nobody knows about them. They lived — and passed away. Many of them were failures — just like me. But God remembers them all — and he can call them by name. When I get discouraged, I go back and read one of those long lists of the sons of Judah or the tribe of Levi. God ain't the changing kind, and I know that somewhere in his lists is old Billy Baker's name."

Most of us are Billy Bakers. We won't splash the headlines — we won't leave our names in history. But we can be faithful and dedicated — just as that secret babysitter was. Only by forgetting ourselves do we discover ourselves.

Remember what Jesus said, "Whosoever will save his life shall lose it; but whosoever shall lose his life (give it away) for my sake and the gospel's, the same shall save it (Mark 8:35)."

A Boy Who
Heard Voices
In The Night

For personal reading: *1 Samuel 1-3*

For public reading: *1 Samuel 3:1-10*

Outline

The Bible Story

A Spiritual Home Is Important

A Personal Experience Is Necessary

A Heavenly Voice Still Speaks

Q-SHEET
A Boy Who Heard Voices In The Night
1 Samuel 1-3

Quiz: *(Match the columns. Try first without a Bible; then use the verses to verify each answer.)*

1. _____ Samuel's father (1:1, 19-20)

2. _____ Samuel's mother (1:20)

3. _____ another wife of Samuel's father (1:2)

4. _____ location of the Lord's house (1:24)

5. _____ priest at the temple there (1:9)

6. _____ son of the priest (1:3)

7. _____ son of the priest (1:3)

8. _____ prayed earnestly for a son (1:11)

9. _____ answered that prayer (1:27)

10. _____ accused Samuel's mother of drunkenness (1:13, 14)

11. _____ means "asked of the Lord" (1:20)

12. _____ Samuel's birthplace (1:19, 20)

13. _____ was "lent to the Lord" (1:28)

14. _____ had long hair (1:11)

15. _____ made Samuel a "little coat" annually (2:19)

16. _____ had three brothers and two sisters (2:21)

17. _____ was becoming blind (3:2; 4:15)

18. _____ called Samuel by name (3:4, 6, 8, 20)

A. Eli
B. Elkanah
C. Hannah
D. Hophni
E. Peninnah
F. Phinehas
G. the Lord
H. Ramah
I. Samuel
J. Shiloh

23

Questions: *(for individual consideration and/or group discussion)*

1. Why was it so important in Bible days for a woman to have children — especially a son (1:11)? How important is it today?

2. Samuel's mother made a promise to God (1:11) and she kept it (1:24-28). What promises have you made to God? Have you kept them all? Why or why not?

3. Why do "good" parents sometimes have "bad" children (2:12, 22-24 — also see 8:3)?

A Boy Who Heard
Voices In The Night

Have you ever had a dream? Have you ever, while you were sleeping, heard someone calling out to you? Have you ever woke up suddenly and wondered whether something actually happened ... whether it was true ... whether it was real?

This Bible story is about a boy like that — a boy who heard voices in the night. It is probably one of the most familiar stories in the Old Testament.

But first, let us go back — even before the birth of this boy — and recall some of the things that had happened (see 1 Samuel 1:1-28; 2:18-21).

A certain man, whose name was Elkanah, was married to two wives. In those days, this was not unusual. One wife's name was Hannah; she had no children. The other wife's name was Peninnah; she had several children. In Bible days, the number of children that a woman had was very important. So it was that Hannah (the wife who did not have any children) felt quite badly — particularly because the other wife teased her and tormented her about it. There must have been a terrific amount of jealousy there.

Again and again, Hannah asked the Lord for a son. One time, when the family had gone to Shiloh — which was the site of the house of the Lord at that time — Hannah went into the temple alone. There she prayed again — earnestly ... fervently ... intensely — that God would give her a son. And she promised, "Lord, if you send me a son, he will belong to you all the days of his life."

The high priest at that time was a man named Eli. And Eli happened to be in the house of the Lord when Hannah was there. As Eli watched Hannah, he became a bit suspicious of her — because he saw that she was moving her lips, but no words were coming out.

So he went over, tapped her on the shoulder, and said, "You shouldn't come into the house of the Lord when you are drunk." And he accused her of being intoxicated.

Hannah tried to explain . . . telling him what she had been doing . . . and insisted that she had not been drinking. She impressed the high priest — and convinced him. As he departed, Eli said, "I will join you in prayer that the Lord will send you the son that you desire."

Within a year, a boy baby was born into Elkanah's home . . . the mother's name was Hannah . . . they were overjoyed. After the baby was born, Hannah named him Samuel — which means "asked of God." And this was certainly true of that baby — he had been requested from the Lord. Now his name, Samuel, indicated that the request had been fulfilled.

Many of us are not aware that our names are important — that they have a meaning. You may not know the meaning of your name — many people don't — but most parents-to-be spend long periods of time, long hours of deep thought, trying to choose the right name for their baby. They want the name to sound right . . . to harmonize with the family name . . . to express their hopes and dreams for their child . . . to represent high standards . . . to inspire certain values . . . to symbolize the right character.

Some time, look up the meaning of your name. Then, learn to live according to your name — try to be the kind of person suggested by your name.

Years ago, there was a soldier in the army of Alexander the Great — the outstanding Greek general who conquered most of the world of his day. The young soldier was caught stealing something from another soldier, and was brought before the famous leader for judgment. The first thing that Alexander the Great asked the man was, "What is your name?"

"Alexander, sir," he answered. He had the same name as his commanding officer — and Alexander means "defender of men."

After reviewing the case and passing sentence, Alexander the Great ordered the soldier: "Go, and change either your name or your character."

26

During the early years of his life, Samuel was tenderly and lovingly cared for, because Hannah devoted her whole life to her baby. Then, when he was still a little boy — probably age three or four — Hannah took him to the temple at Shiloh. She went to Eli, and said, "Do you remember me? From many months ago? You thought I was drunk. I was praying for a son. Here he is. I want you to take him. I want you to keep him. I want him to live in the house of the Lord. I want him to be a servant of God." And she left Samuel with Eli, the high priest. How would you like to live at the church . . . with the pastor . . . all the time . . . 24 hours a day?

I guess we might say that Samuel was sort of a permanent acolyte from that time on. We don't know what all of his duties were, but some of his responsibilities probably were to light candles . . . run errands . . . hold the sacred vessels during the various ceremonies of the temple . . . open and close the doors of the Lord's house. We know that he did this, because it is specifically mentioned in our scripture chapter (1 Samuel 3:15).

Samuel started to serve God at a very young age. Hannah wanted him really to belong to the Lord. So she dedicated her child into God's hands and into God's service. She literally left her son in the Lord's house.

And as far as we know, from the Bible record, she only saw her boy about once a year after that incident. Every year, the family would make the trip to Shiloh. And each time she came to the temple, Hannah would bring a little coat for Samuel — a coat that she herself had made. I can imagine that — every year, as she would travel to the house of the Lord — she would wonder, "How much bigger will Samuel be this year?" She would hope that she had guessed the correct length and right size for the coat.

Year by year, she could see him growing — not only becoming taller and heavier, but also becoming more godly and more holy in his way of life.

Then when he was about 12 years old, Samuel had an overwhelming nighttime experience. By this time, he was no longer just an acolyte — he could be called an assistant priest. He was well acquainted with the temple and its functions ... he knew its rituals and its ceremonies ... he was close to God.

One particular night, after finishing his tasks, he went to bed. As he was sleeping, he heard someone call his name, "Samuel."

Always prompt and obedient, up he jumped ... ran to a nearby room ... woke up Eli ... and asked, "You called me?"

"No, son, I didn't call you. You must have been dreaming. Go on back to bed."

Back to his room Samuel went. But just as he was drifting off to sleep — "Samuel." Sure enough, he was being called again.

Over to Eli's room he went once more. "Here I am — you did call me, sir."

"No, not at all," replied Eli, "I did not call you. Go and lie down."

Then, for the third time, the same thing occurred — "Samuel." This time, he went running over and said to Eli, "I know you called me this time, because I lay awake all the time, waiting to hear the voice. I'm sure you called me."

By this time, Eli realized what was happening. He understood that the Lord himself was trying to get through to the lad ... and he instructed Samuel, "Return to your room, and lie down. When you are called the next time, you answer, 'Speak, Lord, for thy servant heareth.' "

Samuel went back to his room ... back to his bed ... but not back to sleep. Then — for the fourth time — he heard that voice. And this time, it was urgent: "Samuel, Samuel." His name was repeated, "Samuel, Samuel."

There is a compelling, convincing power when you hear your own name twice. For instance, if your mother is trying to call you, and she yells your name once — you may not pay too much attention. But when she shouts your name twice — or when she uses all three of your names — you know that she means business ... that you need to hurry ... that there is no time to dilly-dally.

I can think of only four other places in the Bible where a name is used in this double, repetitive form — and in each case, it is at a critical moment:

1) "Abraham, Abraham" — when he was raising his knife to slay his son on Mount Moriah.

2) "Moses, Moses" — when he was approaching the burning bush on Mount Horeb.

3) "Saul, Saul" — when he was nearing the city of Damascus.

4) "Martha, Martha" — when she was preparing dinner in the village of Bethany.

When the Lord's voice came to Samuel for the fourth time, it was urgent ... pressing ... imperative ... insistent: "Samuel, Samuel."

Samuel answered, as Eli had told him, "Speak, Lord, for thy servant heareth." And that night, the Lord did speak — and Samuel did hear. Coming events were revealed — and certain judgments were pronounced.

As the years passed, Samuel continued to grow in his personal knowledge of the Lord. Eventually, he became an exceptional leader ... an eminent priest ... the last of the excellent judges ... one of the extraordinary prophets of the Lord's people. Judge ... priest ... prophet — the only other person to properly qualify for all three of these titles is our Lord Jesus!

A Spiritual Home Is Important

Many are the lessons to be learned from the life of young Samuel; let us look at three.

The value of a godly home life is impossible to calculate. Samuel would never have become what he was (and who he was) except for the guidance of his mother and father — certainly of his mother.

Hannah shines as a radiant example of motherhood. She was an outstanding model of a righteous, dedicated parent.

"As long as he lives, he will belong to the Lord." Thus she dedicated her son — even before he was born. Thus she dedicated her son — after he was born.

The days in which Samuel lived were evil days. This is obvious as we read the stories in the book of Judges. Wickedness had crept into the life of God's people. It was an age of decadence and depravity ... of immorality and iniquity ... of corruption and cruelty ... of violence and vice ... of lust and lawlessness ... of sin and selfishness and shame.

As we view the permissiveness ... the pornography ... the profanity ... the perversion ... the promiscuity of the days in which we live, it becomes unmistakably clear that we are imitating — and duplicating — the evil days of Samuel.

In this kind of an age, the influence of an upright home is vitally important. How desperately our nation — our generation — needs Christian homes, where God is worshiped devoutly ... where the Savior is exalted dauntlessly ... where prayers are offered daily ... where the scriptures are taught diligently ... where eternal values are honored deliberately ... love is demonstrated dynamically.

Many of you who are parents did dedicate your children. Do you remember your first baby? Do you recall your promises ... your hopes ... your dreams ... your aspirations ... for that child?

Do you still feel that way? It doesn't make any difference what their age is — dedicate your children: unborn ... recently born ... long ago born. Dedicate your children ... dedicate your family ... dedicate your home — to the Lord of lords, the King of kings.

A Personal Experience Is Necessary

A second truth I see in this story is this — in your relationship with God, no one else can substitute for you.

Christianity is a deeply personal and individual matter. Each person needs to meet God for himself or herself. Each person needs to trust the Lord for himself or herself.

Samuel had a wonderful mother ... but he was not saved by his mother's faith. Oh, it helped ... without doubt. But Samuel had to develop his own faith. And — at an appropriate time — the Lord spoke to him, personally.

No one is saved by her mother or father ... by his son or daughter ... by her brother or sister ... by a wife or husband. Frequently, I have somebody tell me, "My father was a pastor; that ought to count for something" or "My brother entered the ministry" or "My daughter is a missionary."

These will not help you — you have your own life to account for, before God. And in the words of Jesus himself, "Except a man be born again, he cannot see the kingdom of God ... Ye must be born again (John 3:3, 7)."

We all need such an experience: personally ... particularly ... privately. Others can help ... others can care ... others can pray ... others can prepare the way ... others can lay the foundations ... others can make it easier — but ultimately we must stand on our own two feet in the presence of God. Christianity is a personal experience.

A Heavenly Voice Still Speaks

A third lesson from this story of Samuel is a very simple — although profound — truth: that God continues to try to communicate with us.

Amid all the noises and clatter of the day, it is a wonder that we ever hear God's voice. But the Lord is still speaking.

How does he speak? In a variety of ways — because he speaks to us as individuals, in a very personal way. He speaks in a different way to you than to me ... he speaks in a different way to you than to your husband or wife ... he speaks in a different way to you than to your friends and neighbors.

The important thing is not how God speaks, but that he is speaking — and that we are listening. Not everybody has the same experience. Not everybody receives the same message in the same way.

Sometimes God speaks through the Bible — it is his letter to us, for guidance . . . strength . . . inspiration . . . comfort.

Sometimes God speaks through prayer. It is a two-way conversation, not a monologue which we direct to the Lord.

Sometimes God speaks through other people — a pastor . . . a parent . . . a teacher . . . a neighbor.

Sometimes God speaks through an inspirational book . . . a work of art . . . great music . . . a meaningful poem . . . a job well done.

Sometimes God speaks through conscience — an inner sense of right and wrong.

Sometimes God speaks through the example of the Lord Jesus Christ — be well acquainted with the four Gospel accounts of his life.

Have you ever been reading a book . . . meditating alone . . . searching the scriptures . . . listening to a sermon . . . or participating in a study group when suddenly you knew — you absolutely and instinctively knew — exactly what God wanted you to do?

Many of us have had that kind of experience. We haven't always been obedient, but there have been times when — just as surely as if we heard a physical voice — God spoke to us.

However he does it, God does still speak. And if we haven't heard him, maybe we are making too much noise. He does not usually shout — rather, he is more apt to whisper. Maybe we need to be still, and know that he is God (see Psalm 46:10). For if we live in such chaotic confusion and hectic haste that we can't hear God when he screams, how can we expect to hear his "still, small voice (1 Kings 17:12)?"

"Breathe through the heats of our desire
    Thy coolness and thy balm;
 Let sense be dumb, let flesh retire:
 Speak through the earthquake, wind, and fire,
    O still, small voice of calm."
                                    — John G. Whittier

A Boy
Who Challenged
A Giant

For personal reading: *1 Samuel 16, 17*

For public reading: *1 Samuel 17:2-11, 32-49*

Outline

The Bible Story

What's Inside Is What Counts

Today's Goliaths

Confront These Giants

Q-SHEET
A Boy Who Challenged A Giant
1 Samuel 16, 17

Quiz: *(Circle the correct word. Try first without a Bible; then use the verses to verify each answer.)*

1, 2. David's home was (Jerusalem, Bethlehem, Jericho), where (Moses, Samuel, Jesus) also was born (16:4-13; Luke 2:4-7).

3-5. David was the (youngest, middle, oldest) son of (Jesse, Abinadab, Saul) and took care of (cooking, his mother, sheep) (16:10-13).

6-8. David had (7, 6, 4) brothers, two of whom were (Ramah, Eliab, Samuel, Shammah, Abner, Jonathan) (16:6, 9).

9, 10. David was anointed with (water, wine, oil) by (Saul, Samuel, Simon) (16:13).

11, 12. The army of Israel prepared to battle the (Midianites, Philistines, Canaanites) in the valley of (Jordan, Jezreel, Elah) (17:2, 19).

13-15. The champion of the enemy army was a giant, named (Goliath, Gath, Genesis), who ridiculed Israel's (women, soldiers, laws) twice daily for (7, 21, 40) days (17:4-11, 16).

16-18. David conquered (Goliath, Gath, Genesis) with a (sword, spear, slingshot), a (staff, shield, stone), and the help of (his brothers, the Lord, artillery) (17:45-50).

34

Questions: *(for individual consideration and/or group discussion)*

1. Why did David select five stones from the brook when he only needed one (17:40)?

2. Fights between chosen representatives of armies were not unusual in ancient times (17:8-10). Might this be a good idea today? Why or why not? Should the champion be a military or a political choice? What problems are really solved by war? Are there some things worse than war? If so, what?

3. On what basis do we ordinarily judge others (16:7)?

A Boy Who Challenged A Giant

The story of David, the shepherd boy, is very well known — but let's review it, because it is always meaningful and exciting.

David was a young, red-headed shepherd boy. This made him different from most people of that particular area — for in the place where David lived, there weren't very many red-headed boys.

He was the youngest of a family that had eight boys — yes, that's right, he had seven older brothers.

His home was the little town of Bethlehem. We remember, at Christmas time, that the angel of the Lord spoke to the astonished shepherds, "Unto you is born this day in the city of David a Savior . . ." The city of David — Bethlehem. That was his home.

As the youngest boy in the family, it was David's job to take care of the few sheep that the family owned. He was a good shepherd. Tending the flock in the hills and the wilderness, with nature on every side of him, David learned to live alone, with his sheep. Outdoors — in the solitude and quietness — he learned how to talk with God. He learned how to listen, too — and hear the voice of God. He came to know God well.

He learned how to sing — and to play his harp. When we think of a harp today, we think of a large musical instrument — so big that it needs a truck to be transported. But David's harp was small — a kind of a lyre, a small instrument, with strings, that could easily be carried around.

He became quite a singer — and he began to compose some poems. You know one of the songs that he wrote, I'm sure:

"The Lord is my shepherd; I shall not want.
He maketh me to lie down in green pastures:
He leadeth me beside the still waters.
He restoreth my soul . . ." (Psalm 23)

36

David realized that just as he took care of his sheep, and met their needs — so the Lord was his shepherd, and was the one who would meet all of his needs.

David was a brave boy. One time, a lion — and another time, a bear — tried to attack some of his lambs. David saved his sheep — and killed the lion and the bear. That's quite a feat for a young shepherd boy — alone.

One day, David was out in the field, taking care of the sheep. He knew that his father and his brothers would be busy that day, because a very special man had come to town — the great prophet named Samuel. Samuel had come to Bethlehem for a religious feast, and Jesse (David's father) and all of David's brothers were invited to attend. So David knew that he was going to be alone all day — but that really wasn't unusual for him. He did feel a little sad that he couldn't go to that special feast — he would have liked to see the famous prophet.

While he was thinking about it — sort of wishing he could be there — he saw somebody in the distance, running across the fields toward him. "Something must have happened," he thought to himself; "That looks like one of my brothers. There's surely something wrong."

He was right. It was one of his brothers. And he came closer and closer, till finally (quite out of breath) he exclaimed, "David ... David ... go on back home. You've got to go back ... right away. The prophet Samuel wants to see you!"

What had happened was that Samuel had come to Bethlehem because God had told him that one of Jesse's sons was to be the next king of Israel. So Samuel examined the family of Jesse. As he looked at the oldest son, he was impressed, and said, "Surely this fine, strong, handsome young man is the one whom the Lord has chosen."

But the voice of God spoke to him and said, "No, Samuel, that is not the one. Remember, man looks on the outward appearance, but the Lord looks on the heart."

So Jesse brought forth his second son. And again God said, "No."

Then the third ... the fourth ... the fifth ... the sixth ... the seventh. And one by one, God said, "No."

Finally, Samuel said to Jesse, "You must have another son, haven't you?"

"Well, just the youngest one ... only a boy. He's out tending the flocks."

"Send for him."

So they sent into the fields for David — and he returned. Immediately — as soon as Samuel saw David — he knew that this was the boy ... the one chosen by God ... the one who would become the next king of Israel.

There, in Bethlehem, Samuel anointed the young shepherd — by pouring olive oil on the top of David's head. The Bible doesn't tell us exactly what happened, but I imagine that Samuel explained to David what it meant. Certainly, that was a great experience in the life of David.

Then time passed by, and David grew up to be a young man ... still tending the sheep ... still the youngest of the family ... still looked down on by his brothers, even though he had been anointed by Samuel. His brothers had almost forgotten about that.

A war was being fought — the armies of Israel were battling the armies of the Philistines. And three of David's brothers were in the army of Israel.

One day, Jesse said to David, "Here, take some food. Go, visit your brothers ... find out if they are well ... leave the food ... and bring me a message from them."

David went forth — and we all remember the story of what happened in the valley of Elah. I wish that sometime you could visit the valley of Elah. It is so easy to picture — as you look up the valley — a great army on the hill to the left ... another great army on the hill to the right ... and the broad flat valley itself, as it widens between the two mountain ranges. It was a natural setting for a battle, in Bible times.

But there was no great struggle between the two armies that day. Everything was quiet and still — until, while David was talking with his brothers, out from the camp of the Philistines came Goliath, a giant more than nine feet tall. His deep voice thundered across the valley: "Send a man to fight me," he roared, "If he defeats me, we will be your servants. But if I prevail, you will serve us."

The soldiers of Israel were terrified. Every morning and every evening — twice a day for 40 days — Goliath had been doing this: challenging and insulting the soldiers ... defying and ridiculing the people of Israel ... mocking and sneering at their God. When David learned what had been happening, he volunteered to go out against the giant.

The king of Israel, a man named Saul, was the logical person to fight Goliath — he stood head and shoulders above any of his soldiers ... he was the tallest ... he was the strongest ... he was the king. Yes, he was the logical one to go — but he was as afraid as anybody else.

When David said, "I will go," Saul insisted, "No, you can't go ... I won't let you ... you're only a boy ... he's a man. He's been fighting all his life ... he will slash you to pieces."

David told Saul how he had killed a lion ... killed a bear ... defended the sheep from other perils ... and had been protected by God. And he concluded, "I will go in the name of the Lord — and that insolent giant shall be slain."

And he talked Saul into allowing him to go. Then Saul wanted to dress him for the fight — placing the largest pieces of heavy armor on little David. "No, I can't wear these," said David, as he laid the armor aside, "I can't even move."

David then went down to the nearby brook — and picked out five smooth stones. In our home, we still have stones from the valley of Elah — because when we were there, our son went down to the brook and picked out five stones. He wanted to be like David.

David also took his slingshot — made simply of a couple of cords, with a leather holder in the center. The idea was to place a stone in the holder ... twirl it around your head once or twice ... release one of the cords ... and discharge the stone.

Even today, shepherd boys in that part of the world know how to use these slingshots. It is possible to become extremely accurate with them. The Bible (Judges 20:16) tells about a band of men who were such skillful sharpshooters that they could split a hair!

You can imagine how accurate David was. He spent much time, out in the fields, practicing with his slingshot. When the sheep were safe and secure, David probably was playing his harp and singing — or practicing with his sling. David was an expert, and Goliath ... with all his height ... with all his power ... with all his heavy armor ... never had a chance. He was never even close enough to touch David. But he didn't realize what was going to happen.

As young David came out to meet him, Goliath looked at him, and cursed, "Who are they sending out here? What do you think I am — a dog? Coming after me with a piece of wood, like that staff. Why, little boy, I'll just rip you to pieces, and throw your flesh all over the valley of Elah."

David stood his ground, and said, "Look, you defy the armies of Israel ... you come to me with a sword and spear and shield ... but I come to you in the name of the living God."

And as Goliath started toward him, David advanced ... whipped out his slingshot ... placed a stone on it ... spun it over his head ... released the stone ... and hit Goliath in the forehead. The stone sank in, and Goliath collapsed — dead. That day, the armies of Israel won a great victory!

And that shepherd boy — years later — became the greatest king that Israel ever knew. If you go to Israel today, one place you will undoubtedly visit is the tomb of King David. For all Jews, it is a holy and sacred spot.

David was such an outstanding leader ... such a celebrated hero ... such a distinguished king ... that the coming Messiah of the Hebrews was to be of "the seed of David" (see Romans 1:3; 2 Timothy 2:8; Revelation 22:16; Isaiah 11:1) ... was to inherit "the throne of David" (see Isaiah 9:7; Luke 1:32) ... was to be called "the son of David" (see Matthew 1:1; 12:23; 21:9; 22:42).

And even today, the insignia of the nation of Israel, the symbol that designates an Israeli, is the six-pointed star — of David!

So this young shepherd — the red-haired boy who tended the sheep — became the man who is noted as one of the most remarkable and most acclaimed Jewish leaders who ever lived.

What's Inside Is What Counts

There are many truths from this story that could be discussed — I wish we had more space and more time to examine them. Let me briefly call three ideas to your attention — then you can amplify them for yourself.

It is still true that "man looketh on the outward appearance, but the Lord looketh on the heart (1 Samuel 16:7)." Samuel was sure that the tall, strong, impressive boy — the oldest son of Jesse — was the person to be the next king.

But the Lord spoke, "Not at all. You examine only the external evidence . . . what is visible to the eye . . . what is often merely a masquerade or camouflage. I look beneath the surface . . . at the essential truth . . . at the core of being. I look on the heart."

We all recognize that what is on the inside is what really matters, and — in our wiser, rational moments — we all recognize that we cannot hide anything from the Lord God Almighty. We might be able to conceal certain actions or attitudes from the preacher . . . from the Sunday school teacher . . . from mother and dad . . . from brothers and sisters . . . from friends and neighbors — but we cannot hide them from God. He looks on the heart; he sees what is there; he knows the truth about us. We cannot deceive him . . . we cannot cheat him . . . we cannot lie to him . . . we cannot keep any secret from him (see Luke 12:2, 3).

41

Today's Goliaths

Many persons today regard giants as relics of the past . . .
as legends . . . as fiction . . . as fables or fairy tales . . . as myths
or fantasies.

The truth is that there are powerful giants in our world
. . . today . . . now. We all meet them — giants who seem impossible to overcome . . . giants that defy the Lord and his
way of life . . . giants that would destroy what is valuable and
virtuous . . . giants that champion the cause of evil . . . giants
that threaten our very existence.

Some of these fiendish monsters are drunkenness and ad-
diction . . . immorality and adultery . . . corruption and bribery
. . . dishonesty and deception . . . lust and perversion.

Such wicked and vicious giants confront us on every side.
They are loose in the world today . . . seeking to enslave us
. . . blaspheming the name of the Lord our God . . . enticing
us from the pathways of righteousness. They are Goliaths —
nine and 10 feet high. We must face them. How can we hope
to overcome them?

Confront These Giants

If you are a Christian — a believer in the living God, a
disciple of the Lord Jesus Christ — plan to face these giants
. . . to challenge them . . . to confront them . . . to do battle
with them . . . to overcome and conquer them.

David believed that God could handle Goliath; he really
believed it. But David didn't therefore relax in his tent and
say, "Okay, God, you go ahead and do it; take care of that
foul-mouthed bully." David ventured forth — he went out and
allowed the Lord to work through him.

So it is today, that when we meet these powerful giants
of evil and wickedness, it isn't enough simply to recline in ease,
trusting in God to take care of them. That isn't faith — it's
laziness. And we have lots of lazy Christians these days, who

need to arise and go forth in the strength of the living God — just as David did: "You come to me with spear and shield . . . with an M-16 and a hand grenade . . . with all the weapons of the world. But I come to you in the name of the Lord of hosts, whom you've defied — the eternal King, whom you've insulted."

Whatever your age — you will be fighting spiritual battles in the days ahead. With a vital, active faith (like David's) and in the power of God, you too can defeat today's giants of wickedness.

A
Little
Lame Prince

For personal reading: *2 Samuel 4:4, 9*

For public reading: *2 Samuel 4:4; 9:1-7*

Outline

The Bible Story

God's Grace

Our Gratitude

A Little Lame Prince
2 Samuel 4:4; 9

Quiz: *(Fill in the blanks. Try first without a Bible; then use the verses to verify each answer.)*

1, 2. Mephibosheth's father was _____; his grandfather was _____ (4:4).

3, 4. Mephibosheth was crippled for life, when he was _____ years old, because his _____ dropped him (4:4).

5-8. _____, the king, learned from _____, a former servant of _____, that Mephibosheth was living at the home of _____ (9:1-5).

9-13. Because Mephibosheth's father, _____, and King _____ had been the closest of friends, Mephibosheth was granted the land of _____, was asked to _____ with the king, and moved to the city of _____ (9:7, 13 — see also 1 Samuel 18:1-4; 20:42).

Questions: *(for individual consideration and/or group discussion)*

1. In what ways is there a parallel between Mephibosheth and the Christian experience? Consider that we were — born to a royal line, but were crippled by a fall (4:4; Genesis 1:26, 27; 3); in exile from the King, and were remembered because of a covenant (9:7; Hebrews 13:20); exalted because of the merits of another (9:1-7; 1 John 2:12); given a glorious inheritance (9:9; 1 Peter 1:4).

2. Why should we be forgiving, compassionate, merciful (9:1, 6, 7)? What does it do for others? What does it do for us?

3. What can I do to help those who cannot help themselves — the lame, the blind, the deaf, the homeless (9:7, 8)?

A Little Lame Prince

Once upon a time, there lived in a beautiful palace a king — a king whose name was Saul. The king's son also lived in the same palace — his name was Jonathan. The king also had a grandson — Jonathan's son — who was a little boy with a big name. His name was Mephibosheth. That's a tongue-twister, isn't it? It is a hard name to spell — and it is as hard to pronounce as it is to spell: Mephibosheth (Mĕh - fĭh - bō - shĕth). At the time we meet him, he was about five years old.

One morning his father and grandfather (Jonathan and Saul) came to him and said, "Good-bye." They were going off to war. That was the last time the boy saw his father and grandfather alive. Saul and Jonathan both died during the battle. Two of Jonathan's brothers, uncles of young Mephibosheth, were also slain. It was a terrible day for the people of Israel, God's people.

When the news reached the palace, there was terror. Everyone was not only upset and worried — they were terribly frightened. They realized that as soon as the Philistines ... the enemies of God's people ... who had won the battle ... arrived at the palace, they would surely kill anyone they could get their hands on ... all of the servants ... and multitudes of others, as well. Everybody began to pack up and run — there was a lot of hurry and much panic.

Now a little five-year-old boy can't run very fast, and a little five-year-old boy can't run very far. Mephibosheth got tired. He began to cry. He couldn't understand all the haste, all the rush.

So his nurse, who was caring for him, swished him up into her arms, laid him across her shoulder, and tried to run while carrying him as well.

She had not run very far before she realized how heavy he was, and as she tried to adjust his weight on her shoulder, she stumbled — and dropped the prince!

Mephibosheth fell to the ground, hurting both feet so badly that he was a cripple for the rest of his life. He was never able to walk and run and play, as other boys did.

Eventually, he was taken to the other side of the river Jordan, to the house of a kind man named Machir, who cared for him as time passed by and the boy grew.

This is about all we know about the little lame prince, as a boy. And, really, I have sort of polished up the story, because the Bible doesn't tell all of this. I'm not sure that it happened exactly this way. We do know that Mephibosheth was five years old . . . we do know that his nurse dropped him . . . we do know when it happened — the day his father and grandfather were killed in the battle . . . we do know that he was lame for the rest of his life.

As the years passed, another man (a man named David, a very close friend of Mephibosheth's father) organized an army and drove the Philistines out of the promised land. Finally, that man became the king of Israel.

When David had established himself on the king's throne, he wondered if any members of Jonathan's family were still alive. He remembered his abiding friendship with Jonathan — he and Jonathan had been bosom pals.

He sent out search parties. They scouted everywhere . . . and finally the word came back, "Yes, a servant of Saul had been located." His name was Ziba.

The servant was called in, and David asked, "Is there anybody left, anybody at all, of Saul's family?"

"Yes, Jonathan had a son, a son who is still alive. He's lame, lame on both feet."

"Where is he? Do you know?" And when David learned where Mephibosheth was, he sent for him and had him ushered into the throne room.

When Mephibosheth entered, he was scared. That's why David said, "Fear not."

Kings usually, in those days, executed any member of the family that had preceded them, so that nobody . . . able to claim the throne — would remain. The easiest way to keep anybody from trying to take away your crown was — get rid of him before he caused problems.

So Mephibosheth just figured that David had searched for him ... finally caught up with him ... and was going to slay him.

David assured him, "No, you don't need to be afraid. Mephibosheth, I loved your father, Jonathan. He was my closest friend. And because of him, I want to restore your inheritance — the property which belonged to your family.

"And I want you to come and live with me, in the palace ... for your father's sake, for Jonathan's sake. I really want you to dwell in the royal palace ... to eat at the royal table ... to be part of the royal family."

And Mephibosheth, the Bible very clearly says, was still lame — still crippled in both feet.

That's the story — it isn't very long, but it has many lessons for us to remember. Let us consider two.

God's Grace

David's kindness and generosity were extraordinary and unusual. In that time, the normal procedure would have been for David to put to death any possible claimant to the throne: Jonathan's brothers and sisters ... all of their children ... indeed, every member of the family of Saul.

David was not required to show any mercy to Mephibosheth at all. In fact, just the opposite was expected.

Why, then, did he act as he did? Simply because of Jonathan. Mephibosheth did not do anything to earn or to deserve such kindness. But David — for the sake of Jonathan — restored Mephibosheth, made him a part of the royal family. He did it in consideration of another.

As great as the unselfish generosity of David was, the grace of God is even greater, infinitely greater. You see, we too belonged to a royal line ... were crippled by a fall ... and, in our sin, fled from the presence of the King of kings.

But he sought us out. Jesus came into the world "to seek and to save that which was lost (Luke 19:10)." In his love and compassion, he searched for us — and found us — in order that he might restore our inheritance, "an inheritance incorruptible, and undefiled, and that fadeth not away, reserved in heaven" for those of us who are kept, by faith, in his salvation (1 Peter 1:4).

When we had fled from him, God pursued us . . . called us into his presence . . . exalted us because of the merits of another . . . and restored our glorious inheritance.

We did not deserve this. We were not worthy of it. We did nothing to merit it.

Many times, in my preaching, I have said, "If we got what we deserved, we would all go to hell." That would be justice. Justice is giving a person what he deserves. But I do not seek justice from God. If I got what I deserved, I would go to hell.

Is there anyone who deserves to go to heaven? Is there anyone who has been good enough . . . kind enough . . . loving enough . . . obedient enough . . . perfect enough . . . holy enough? Who has earned the right to enter into the courts of eternal glory?

A favorite story of mine is about a mother who had a son in the army of Napoleon. Her son had been caught in a crime, arrested and sentenced to die. Before the execution, the mother sought to plead for the life of her son — and was granted an audience with the emperor himself.

After her plea, Napoleon responded, "But this is his second offense — justice demands that he die."

Her reply was, "But I do not ask for justice — I plead for mercy."

"But he does not deserve mercy."

"Please, sir, if he deserved it, it wouldn't be mercy!"

And Napoleon was so stirred that he granted the mother's request and spared the life of her son.

All we can do before God, the King of kings, is to ask for mercy (not justice) — plead for it. Then — not because of what we have done, but for the sake of another — it is granted to us.

We usually conclude the prayers we offer with such phrases as "in Jesus' name" or "for Jesus' sake." That is a sacred way to express a prayer or a desire.

Of all the profanity and blasphemy that I hear (so frequently and openly these days), the one that hurts me most is when somebody says, in a very irreverent manner, "for Christ's sake." To the Christian, this phrase is so meaningful ... so holy ... so profound.

God has done so much for us — in granting forgiveness ... deliverance ... sonship ... the riches of his glory. And he has done it, not because we have deserved it; he has done it — for Christ's sake. Just as David showed kindness to Mephibosheth for Jonathan's sake, so the Lord God Almighty grants his infinite grace to us — for Jesus' sake.

We need to remember that through his whole experience Mephibosheth remained "lame on both his feet (9:15)." He fell, as a five-year-old boy, and was crippled. He was still lame when David found him. And in the final passage where he is mentioned, he was still lame (2 Samuel 19:26). His feet were never healed.

So we are constantly crippled by the effects of sin upon our lives. Yes, God cleanses ... forgives ... and restores. But there are certain effects of sin that still remain: the permanent scars from a drunken brawl ... the blinded eye from a brutal fight ... the missing finger from a broken whiskey bottle ... the diseased lungs from too much nicotine ... the damaged liver from too much alcohol ... the deteriorating brain from too many drugs. Sin leaves marks that may never be erased — even for a redeemed and transformed person.

Our Gratitude

Try to imagine how thankful Mephibosheth must have felt. He came into the court, expecting to lose his life. Instead, he became a prince again! He was to live in the palace, be part of the royal family ... eat at the royal table ... be clothed in royal robes. How grateful he must have been! I feel certain that Mephibosheth was willing to do anything possible to please the king, King David, whom he must have loved with all his heart.

Isn't that the way we should be? When we realize how gracious and loving God, the King of kings, has been, aren't we thankful? And don't we want to do whatever we can to show our appreciation?

The story is told that the king of a small country was walking among his people in disguise. He was attracted to a particular beggar, a young pauper who daily was outside the gates of the palace, begging.

The king went to the beggar, identified himself, and said, "I want you to come into the palace and be part of my family. I want to adopt you as my son. I want to make you a prince."

I can picture the beggar scratching his head suspiciously ... wondering what was happening ... deciding whether to believe it. But certainly, if he had a chance to go into the palace, he was going to go. So he entered the palace with the king, who directed the servants to make him a prince.

First, his old, dirty clothes were removed and he was prepared for a bath. "Bath!" he shouted, "Why, I haven't had a bath since — I can't even remember when I had my last bath."

"But you're a prince now. You're living in a palace and you're expected to be clean."

Then he was provided with new clothing — rich, flowing, royal robes — to replace his shabby rags. He didn't really feel very comfortable in such splendid, majestic garments. But he wore them — because he was a prince now.

Soon it was time for dinner. He was ushered to an immense table, far larger than any he had ever seen. When he sat down, he saw countless pieces of silverware — and an abundance of plates and dishes, of all sizes and shapes. He looked around to the attendant standing behind him, and whispered, "What do I do with all these? I've never seen anything like this before."

"But you've never been a prince before, either," the servant reminded him.

Now the point is this: Would not that tramp have been an ungrateful rascal if he had not been willing to learn to live like a prince? Suppose he had refused to take a bath ... suppose he had rejected the royal clothing ... suppose he had said, "I'm going to eat with my fingers, the way I always have." He might have forfeited his princely position.

This illustrates our relationship with God. Our King has removed our filthy rags ... bestowed upon us riches far beyond anything we ever dreamed ... brought us into a heavenly palace ... made us members of his royal family.

Certainly, our lives are different — vastly different — from all that we've known. But how ungrateful we are if we do not try to live as children of God ought to live.

And learning to walk the Christian life is not always easy. It's more difficult than taking a bath for the first time in years. It's more difficult than learning how to handle knives and forks and spoons. But in thanksgiving for the grace of God, how can we do less than make a determined effort to live like a prince or a princess?

———————

Our biblical story for this chapter has been from the Old Testament, but let me conclude with a quotation from the New Testament: "Behold, what manner of love the Father hath bestowed upon us, that we should be called the children of God (1 John 3:1)."

Now put the emphasis on the pronouns: "Behold, what manner of love the Father hath bestowed upon *us,* that *we* (of all people, the least deserving), that *we* should be called the children of God."

Now claim the pronouns — and the promise — for your very own: "Behold, what manner of love the Father hath bestowed upon *me,* that *I* should be called a child of God!"

Part II — Elisha And Some Children

Two Brothers Who Solved An Energy Crisis

For personal reading: *2 Kings 4:1-7*

For public reading: *2 Kings 4:1-7*

Outline

The Bible Story

The Creditor Is Come

What Hast Thou?

Shut The Door

A Blank Check

Two Brothers Who Solved An Energy Crisis
2 Kings 4:1-7

Quiz: *(Circle the correct word. Try first without a Bible; then use the verses to verify each answer.)*

1, 2. Two brothers faced poverty after their father, who (feared the Lord, loved to gamble, had a dangerous job), (left home, lost all his earnings, died) (4:1).

3, 4. Because the two brothers were in danger of becoming (junkies, slaves, soldiers), their mother came to the (king, hospital, prophet) for help (4:1).

5. The family's only possession was (a piece of silver, an old cart, a pot of oil) (4:2).

6-8. The two brothers were sent to the (city, neighbors, general store) to (beg, borrow, steal) as many (empty, small, painted) containers as possible (4:3).

9-11. With the door (broken, repaired, shut), the two brothers kept bringing the vessels to (the prophet, the creditor, their mother), who (prayed over them, poured into them, played music with them) (4:4, 5).

12-14. The two brothers were spared when the (man of God, bank, governor) told their mother to sell the (old cart, home, oil) and pay their (mortgage, income tax, debt) (4:7).

Questions: *(for individual consideration and/or group discussion)*

1. Why is it so often true that moral, righteous, honest, respectable people suffer hardships and afflictions (4:1)? It would seem that they ought to be rewarded, but life doesn't always work out that way. Indeed, sometimes they endure additional pain and adversity because they are pure and upright. Consider the example of Jesus. Is this fair? Why do you think so?

2. What would happen in today's credit-card culture if children could be sold to pay off a debt (4:1)? Would people be more or less likely to abuse their credit? What effect would this have on the number of bankruptcies? In what ways are children sold today?

3. How do you define a miracle (4:5, 6)? What miracles, if any, are still occurring in our scientific, materialistic, technological 20th century?

Two Brothers Who Solved An Energy Crisis

In the land of Israel, there once lived a well-known prophet ... a man of God ... a leader of the people. His name was Elisha.

He was famous throughout the land, and a number of younger prophets were his assistants and helpers: working with him ... serving under him ... ministering to him ... learning from him. They might be called disciples, followers, pupils or apprentices.

One of these "sons of the prophets" was a capable, promising young man with a lovely wife and two attractive children. The two boys in that family enjoyed running and playing together ... doing their chores ... learning their lessons. Though they were poor, they were happy and cheerful.

But a great sorrow came to that home. The father became sick; he grew steadily weaker; and finally died, leaving behind a widow — a mother with two young boys.

That was trouble enough, but because of the sickness and because of their poverty, there were many debts — bills that needed to be paid. And the mother did not have the money.

One day a very stern, rich man came to the home and said, "You must pay what you owe. If you do not pay it by this time next week (the Bible doesn't say it quite this way, but I think that is about what he must have said), I'm going to take your two boys ... sell them into slavery ... and use the money to satisfy your debt."

The mother was terrified ... broken-hearted ... frantic. There was no possible way that she could ever pay the bills. And she just couldn't give up her sons. She was desperate. Finally she went to Elisha, the man of God. She told him what had happened, and asked, "What can I do?"

Elisha thought about the problem, and said, "What do you have? How much do you own? What can you do for yourself?"

She replied, "I don't really have anything except just a small pot of oil." The oil that she had was probably olive oil.

In those days, as today, oil was vital in many different ways. It was used for cooking . . . for illumination and light . . . for heat . . . for medicine . . . for consecration. It was even used (by the rich people) for bathing. It was needed for many different reasons; it was essential to their way of life.

And it was expensive — as it is today. Poor families could not afford to keep a supply of oil.

When the mother said that all she had was one little pot of oil, Elisha told her what to do.

She returned home, called her two boys together, and instructed them, "I want you to go out to our neighbors — you (pointing to one son) go in one direction, and you (speaking to his brother) go the other way. I want you to borrow all the empty jars . . . all the pots and pans . . . all the bottles and jugs . . . all the containers and vessels . . . that the neighbors will let you have."

Imagine the two brothers, scurrying off in two directions . . . telling their neighbors they wanted to borrow empty vessels . . . wondering, I'm sure, whether their mother was a little bit out of her mind.

At last, in obedience to what the man of God had said, they gathered all the empty vessels they had and closed the door.

Then the mother took her small pot of oil — and began to pour it into another container. The boys, with their eyes opening wide, watched in astonishment as their mother poured from the small pot — into a large, tall jar. And it was filled! It was overflowing!

"Hurry," the mother ordered, "Bring me another vessel. Quickly."

One brother carried away the full jar . . . the other brought an empty one . . . and the mother kept on pouring. And the oil continued to flow from the little pot — filling one container after another. The boys had never seen that much oil in their whole lives.

How hard the brothers worked: bringing the empty vessels to their mother . . . carrying away the heavy . . . full ones . . . setting them to one side . . . keeping everything in order.

Finally, their mother said, "Bring me another jar."

And the boys said, "There are no more."

Then the stream of oil stopped. And the widow still had oil in her own small pot!

Elisha, the prophet, then told her what to do, "Take the oil and sell it . . . pay off your debt . . . and there will be enough left over so that you and your sons can live for the rest of your lives."

What a happy ending! Two boys — two brothers — were saved from slavery and from starvation. We can picture the mother, with tears of joy in her eyes, throwing her arms around her two sons and hugging them lovingly.

―――――――

True enough, this is a miracle. But what is your definition of a miracle?

An olive seed has a teeny little bit of oil in it. We can plant it . . . watch it grow . . . and eventually harvest an immense quantity of oil.

Is this a miracle? Why not? Is it any less a miracle because the process takes years instead of hours? It is the Lord who can increase the tiny bit of oil in an olive seed and produce thousands of quarts . . . or gallons . . . or barrels. The same God who can multiply the oil in years can multiply it in hours, if he desires. Why not? It is his creation.

Now let's take a look at some of the events that happened in this particular miracle — there are several matters for us to consider.

The Creditor Is Come

No one is exempt from having troubles. All persons have their share.

This young preacher was a good man . . . his wife was a good woman . . . the two boys were good boys. Yet they faced all kinds of problems and difficulties. Nobody escapes hardship . . . misfortune . . . sorrow . . . pain . . . affliction.

Sometimes we look at rich people and think, "Wouldn't it be nice to have all that money and not have any distress or worry?" But they too have their sufferings and anxieties. We really don't know about their trials, their griefs, their adversities. The American Indians might say, "Don't judge another man's troubles until you've walked in his moccasins for two months."

Even the kindest, the purest, the best, the holiest of people have their anguish ... their suffering ... their burdens ... their calamities. Look at the prophets; look at the saints; look at Jesus himself. Who could have been any better, any holier? Yet what happened? He ended up on a cruel cross, tortured and tormented, with nails through his hands and feet. No one can avoid trouble.

Not until her sons were threatened did this widow cry out for help. We have no way of knowing how many problems she had faced ... how many obstacles she had overcome ... how many heartaches she had endured, without complaining, during the time of her husband's sickness and death — until finally the creditor arrived and said, "I'm going to take away your sons."

That was the last straw. She could face many difficulties ... endure much suffering ... cope with constant poverty and hardship. But for her boys to become slaves — that was the breaking point.

And she could do nothing to prevent it. She had reached a dead end. She was desperate ... helpless ... alone ... forsaken. She was completely unable to pay the bills; there was no possible way; she must have some help from outside.

And so she called on the man of God. And through Elisha, she was calling on the Lord himself.

Maybe we should not wait till the last minute, but when we reach that time of trial and tribulation, this is the proper place to go. God is a very present help in time of trouble, our refuge and our strength (Psalm 46:1); he is our rock and our fortress (Psalm 18:2). Again and again, the Bible tells us that he is the one to whom we should turn, the one upon whom we should depend.

What Hast Thou?

When the widow came to the man of God, it would have been so easy, so logical for him to have reached into his purse and given her some coins. But he didn't.

Or he might have made some visits and collected enough money to pay what she owed. But he didn't.

His first response was a question, "What do you have? How much can you help yourself? Are you going to contribute anything?"

This is important. Miracles occur when men and God work together. We can't perform miracles by ourselves, and God chooses not to — in most cases. He prefers to use human partners.

Faith is no excuse for laziness. Faith does not sit back complacently and say, "All right, God, I believe — now you take care of the problem." Faith is cooperating with God. Together, we and the Lord can produce miracles.

Remember the familiar story of the pastor who was visiting a prosperous farmer? As they talked on the front porch and looked out across the beautiful, rolling countryside, the pastor commented, "You and the Lord have certainly done wonders with this land."

The farmer turned and replied, "But you should have seen it when the Lord had it by himself!"

That's the way life is. There are many things that God does not do — except as he works through us. We depend on God, but God also depends on us. That's when miracles take place.

"What do you have?" the prophet asked. It was only a small pot of oil, but the mother offered it to the Lord — all of it. She held back nothing.

"What do you have?" the Lord is asking. It may not be much, either — but offer it to God. Whatever it is, small as it

62

seems — give it to God. Yes, give it to God ... all of it ... with no strings attached ... now. Complete consecration works miracles!

This woman not only had an active faith and a total dedication, but also a wonderful sense of obedience. She did what Elisha requested. He had instructed her, "Go out and borrow empty vessels. Take your tiny little jar of oil ... and start to pour." How would you react if I told you to do something like that?

But this mother trusted — not only Elisha, but the Lord whom Elisha represented. And she obeyed. The well-loved hymn summarizes the whole gospel in two words — "Trust and Obey."

We need to obey the commandments of God, even though they sometimes seem strange or perplexing. His commandments are given for our benefit ... for our guidance ... for our welfare. We need to follow them no matter how puzzling or difficult they seem. Ours is not to question; ours is to obey.

Shut The Door

Elisha inserted another interesting little direction that I think is significant. He explained, "After you gather the vessels together, shut the door."

"Shut the door." Why? Because there are some experiences of life that are so sacred ... so holy ... so precious that the curious gaze of an unsympathetic public should not witness them. There are some matters — many, in fact — that God handles privately ... intimately ... behind closed doors ... in reverence ... in stillness ... in solitude. Close the door, shut out the world and meet God face to face.

Then when the widow started to pour, she reminds us that the only limitation on the abundance of God is the limitation that we ourselves put upon it.

The only limitation on that flowing oil was the number of empty vessels that she had. Had there been more containers, that little jar would have continued to pour. The oil stopped flowing only when there was no vessel to receive it!

Isn't it remarkable to realize that in the holy scriptures, oil is a symbol of the Holy Spirit? And the Holy Spirit stops flowing only when there are no empty hearts to receive his riches ... no empty souls hungering and thirsting after righteousness ... no empty lives yearning for divine peace and power.

A Blank Check

This account of the two brothers and their mother is another illustration of the amazing grace of our God.

Look at us: we are hopelessly in debt ... destitute ... unable to pay ... in complete despair ... about to perish.

Then in desperation, we cry out to the Lord ... give him what little we have ... faithfully obey his orders.

And in his infinite love and grace, he satisfies our needs — in overflowing abundance.

We bring to him empty vessels — with nothing of self in them. We eliminate self ... bring an empty life to God ... and wait to be filled. And he fills that empty life — with "good measure, pressed down, and shaken together, and running over (Luke 6:38)."

———

There are many New Testament texts for this Old Testament story. Let me remind you of one in particular — the promise given through St. Paul, the apostle, to the Philippian believers: "My God shall supply all your need, according to his riches in glory, by Christ Jesus (Philippians 4:19)."

To me, that's a blank check. Yes, a blank check, signed by the Creator of the universe. Repeat it — slowly: "My God ... shall supply ... all your need ... according to his riches in glory ... by Christ Jesus."

64

Now translate and revise it into the form of a check. For whom? Pay to the order of (insert your own name here). It's for you!

For how much? Enough to satisfy every need of life — "all your needs."

On what bank? Drawn on the treasury of heaven — "his riches in glory."

By whose authority? Signed, The Almighty God, "by Christ Jesus," his only Son, our Lord.

There it is — a blank check. For you. "God shall supply all your need, according to his riches in glory, by Christ Jesus."

Now go out and cash it — not at the bank on Main Street, but at the Bank of Glory, whose eternal resources are unlimited (they never run out).

Our God "is able to do exceedingly abundantly above all that we ask or think (Ephesians 3:20)." How remarkable! Think about it:

He is able to do: All that we ask or think. And even more! Above all that we ask or think. And even more!! Abundantly above all that we ask or think. And even more!!! Exceedingly abundantly above all that we ask or think!!!!

Isn't that incredible! That's what your God is able to do. Have you an energy crisis . . . a financial crisis . . . a family crisis . . . a personal crisis . . . a spiritual crisis . . . any crisis? Here is your answer — God. Yes, God himself, the Almighty Creator, the Lord of Life. Come to him . . . now . . . with an empty heart . . . and wait to be filled.

A Boy
Of Seven
Sneezes

For personal reading: *2 Kings 4:8-37*

For public reading: *2 Kings 4:32-37*

Outline

The Bible Story

Truths To Teach

A Portrait Of Jesus

A Boy Of Seven Sneezes
2 Kings 4:8-37

Quiz: *(True or False? Try first without a Bible; then use the verses to verify each answer.)*

1. _____ This boy's home was the village of Shunem (4:8, 17).

2. _____ His mother and father arranged a special room in the basement for Elisha (4:9, 10).

3. _____ The birth of the boy was a "thank you" from the prophet (4:12-17).

4. _____ The boy went to the harvest field with his father (4:18).

5. _____ There he suffered an extremely severe headache (4:19).

6. _____ His father took the boy to the emergency room (4:19).

7. _____ At midnight, the boy died (4:20).

8. _____ The boy's mother placed his body on Elisha's bed (4:21, 32).

9. _____ His mother then sought Elisha at Mount Carmel (4:25).

10. _____ The prophet gave his staff to his servant, Gehazi, and sent him ahead (4:29).

11. _____ The man of God went alone into the room where the boy lay (4:33).

12. _____ Elisha then closed the door and prayed (4:33).

13. _____ Elisha knelt beside a chair and earnestly exhorted the Lord (4:34).

14. _____ Elisha laid himself upon the boy's body twice (4:34, 35).

15. _____ The boy demonstrated his return to life by eating food (4:35).

Questions: *(for individual consideration and/or group discussion)*

1. How often do we take positive actions or perform generous deeds, just for themselves with no thought of reward, compensation, or recognition (4:9, 10)? What such actions have you taken? Be specific.

2. What do we mean when, in the Apostles' Creed, we affirm our belief in "the resurrection of the body (4:34, 35)?"

3. When calamity strikes, where can we go for help (4:25)? Name as many available resources as you can.

A Boy Of Seven Sneezes

A woman once lived, with her husband, in the little village of Shunem, which lies at the southeast edge of the great valley of Jezreel — sometimes called the plain of Esdraelon; sometimes, Armageddon. It goes by different names.

In that area, much history had originated, even at that time ... more history has originated, since that time ... and yet more history will be originated — because this is where the final, terrible conflict (the battle of Armageddon) will be fought. There, in the small village of Shunem, lived this particular woman.

The Bible says that she was a great woman. The meaning of that word, in the original language, is very simply that she was a well-known, influential and prominent person — a leader in the community and probably quite wealthy.

She was also a very hospitable woman. Apparently, when strangers came into town, they would stop at her home. There they would be invited to partake of food — even to stay overnight.

One day, Elisha the prophet traveled through this village and enjoyed a meal with her family. He was impressed with them; and it became normal for him, as he traveled back and forth through the valley of Jezreel, to visit at this home frequently.

Finally, the woman said to her husband, "I think this man is a holy man, a man of God. Maybe we ought to do something special for him. Since he comes quite often, why don't we add a little room to our house? Then whenever he comes, he can have a private place to stay."

The usual picture we have of this is one of an upper room — a room on top of the house, with an outside stairway. You've seen pictures of Bible homes like this or perhaps you've even been in the Holy Land and seen this kind of addition. Rather than add to the side, they built an upper room on top of the house. Such a small room (a "chamber") was constructed especially for the prophet Elisha.

Still today, when ministers ... church officials ... evangelists ... or missionaries ... are away from home and stay overnight with a local family, they are said to stay in the "prophet's chamber." Elisha deeply appreciated the hospitality of this family. He greatly valued the opportunity to just stop in, whenever he wished, day or night — and find a bed, a desk or small table, a stool and candlesticks. It was a room he could call his own. He was extremely grateful for the woman's thoughtfulness and generosity in providing such a room for his privacy ... his security ... his lodging.

He wanted to express his thanks, so he said to his servant, "Call in the woman, the Shunammite woman." (Apparently it was not proper etiquette, back in those days, for women to talk with men privately; they carried on a conversation by way of somebody else. So Gehazi, the servant, stood in the doorway and relayed the information back and forth.)

"Ask her what we can do for her," Elisha said, "because we appreciate all that she has done for us."

And Gehazi repeated her reply, "Oh, no, I want nothing. I didn't do this because I expected any pay ... any reward ... any recompense. I have everything I need."

Elisha answered, "Can't I put in a good word for you at the court? Wouldn't you like to meet the king? Or the general of the army?" It seems that Elisha had many influential contacts.

But she said, "No, I'm perfectly satisfied, completely content with my life here." Such a spirit of humility and happiness!

Later on, Elisha and his servant were talking about what they might do for the lady and her husband, when Gehazi said, "I've noticed that there aren't any children around the home ... and apparently they haven't any children who are grown ... and her husband is old, so it doesn't seem as if they will have any."

"Call the woman," said Elisha. And again, Gehazi called the woman of Shunem.

Elisha spoke, "About this time next year, you and your husband will become parents — of a son."

"Oh, you're a holy man; you're a man of God," she exclaimed, "Please don't lie to me. This is impossible."

"I do not lie," said Elisha, "It will happen."

In about a year, a baby boy was born into that home, amid much happiness and rejoicing. You can easily imagine this wealthy woman showering her attention ... her love ... her compassion ... her tenderness ... upon this baby. She was very grateful — because she loved children so much.

Over a period of time, the child grew, reared in an atmosphere of devotion ... concern ... tenderness ... and holiness. The son was probably nine or 10, possibly 12 years old when the next incident happened. (Commentators give varying estimates about the age of the boy — and the scriptures don't tell us ... so we just have to guess.)

He was old enough, however, to go with his father out to the field. And it was the time of the reaping — harvest time. The son apparently wasn't big enough to help (very much, anyhow) but he was old enough to go along with his father — and play.

This particular morning, he coaxed his dad to take him to the field. And the father agreed, "All right, come along."

So the boy went, and spent the morning running and playing in the field, stopping occasionally to work a little bit.

It was a hot day, and at length the boy came running to his dad and complained, "My head! My head!" He was sick — very sick.

His father tried to help him, then finally called one of the servants and said, "Take him to his mother."

A typical dad. "Take him to his mother." You mothers should be complimented that most men feel this way. Sometimes you may not appreciate it, but when there is real trouble, that's a normal male reaction: "Take the boy to his mother — she'll know what to do."

The servant picked up the lad — and hurried back to the home, where the mother took the boy upon her lap. She did everything she could, but the Bible tells us that at noon, the boy died — apparently of sunstroke, sunstroke from the heat of the day.

The mother, of course, was heartbroken. After all, this was a miracle child — a child of promise ... a child of hope ... a child of prayer ... a child of dreams.

And now — he was gone ... unexpectedly ... suddenly ... swiftly. Laughing and running and playing one hour. A short time later — lifeless. So it is that death can strike: quickly ... without warning ... like a bolt from the blue.

But the mother was not panic-stricken. She maintained her courage and her faith. She lifted her son ... carried him to Elisha's room ... laid his body on the prophet's bed ... and sent a message to her husband, asking for a servant and a donkey, saying that she was going to see the man of God.

Her husband (not knowing the boy was dead) was surprised and bewildered. "This is no sabbath or holy day," he said, "This is no special occasion. Why go to see the prophet?"

Her only answer was, "Shalom," which literally means "Peace." The Bible says, "It shall be well."

Why did she say "Shalom" when she knew her son was dead? Why did she not tell her husband of the boy's death? Why did she say "Peace" when I'm sure there was no peace in her own heart? We really don't know the answers to these questions, but somehow or other, she may have felt that the same prophet who had made it possible for her to have this child would make it possible for her to keep this child.

So she and a servant hurried to find the prophet. She said, "Now you drive forward as fast as you can; don't wait up for me, unless I absolutely insist." And they started up the valley of Jezreel toward Mount Carmel.

From a distance, Elisha saw them. He realized who it was, and sent his servant to ask the woman, "Is it well with thee? Is it well with thy husband? Is it well with the child?"

Her reply was, "Shalom." There is that word again. "Shalom" — "Peace" — "It is well."

You can remember that word, "Shalom," by recalling that Jerusalem is called the City of Peace and in Hebrew, it is "Yeru - shalom" (City of Peace).

72

Why did the woman say, "It is well," when she knew that her son was lying dead? We don't know. Nobody really knows. She might have had faith that it was going to be well. Or maybe she didn't want to talk to Gehazi — but she wanted to see Elisha himself. At any rate, that is what happened. She came to the prophet ... dropped at his feet ... and started to speak. (I feel sure that she had a speech all planned in her mind.)

"Did I ask you for a son?" she began. "Didn't you give him to me of your own free will? Didn't I ask you not to lie to me?"

And then, abruptly ... her speech ended. I believe that she had other words she wanted to speak — but I'm guessing that her voice broke. You've had that happen, haven't you? Filled with strong emotion, you tried to say something, and you just choked up and could not speak at all. I think that may be what happened here.

Elisha sensed what had happened, and said to Gehazi, "Here, take my staff and run ahead — and lay it on the boy."

Gehazi took the staff, went ahead, placed it on the boy — to no avail.

He turned ... came running back ... met them on the way ... and said, "It's no use."

Why didn't the staff work? Again, we don't know. Maybe that kind of power can't be transferred. Maybe there is no miracle-working power in a staff. Maybe Elisha was only confirming the boy's death. We don't know the reason — but Elisha came ... went up to his own room ... and saw the boy on the bed.

He stretched himself out on top of the boy: mouth to mouth ... eyes to eyes ... hands to hands. Talk about mouth-to-mouth resuscitation! It isn't a modern 20th century discovery; it goes, at least, far back before the time of Christ into the days of the Old Testament.

Elisha breathed into the boy's mouth ... prayed deeply and earnestly and felt the body begin to get warm. He arose ... walked a little ... prayed some more ... laid back down on the boy ... and gave him further resuscitation.

Then it happened! "Ah-choo! . . . Ah-choo! . . . Ah-choo!" Three . . . four . . . five . . . six . . . seven sneezes! Seven times the boy sneezed — his eyes opened — and life was back in his body!

Elisha called Gehazi and said, "Tell the woman to come." She came at once. Elisha said, "Take up your son."

She dropped at the feet of the man of God, tears streaming down her cheeks, trying to say, "Thank you."

What a happy ending! What a touching story!

Truths To Teach

Several subjects could be emphasized here — to demonstrate the meaning of the story and allow it to be helpful for us.

We could learn about hospitality — because this is a Christian virtue. How meaningful it is for a Christian to be kind . . . friendly . . . open-hearted . . . accommodating . . . helpful . . . thoughtful . . . generous. All of this is seen in the attitudes and the actions of the woman of Shunem — and wherever we find Christianity being practiced.

We could learn about faith — again, as embodied in this woman. How firm and courageous . . . steadfast and constant . . . resolute and unwavering . . . was her faith in the midst of difficult circumstances and grievous trials. She never gave up. Her hope was always alive.

We could learn about eternal life — because resurrection is a central message of this incident. Death is not the end. God's power and presence extend beyond the grave.

We could learn about prayer — and its power. The child was a result of prayer. He was reared in an atmosphere of prayer. And it was prayer that restored him to life.

"The effectual, fervent prayer of a righteous man availeth much (James 5:16)."

"More things are wrought by prayer than this world dreams of." — Tennyson, *Morte d'Arthur*

A Portrait Of Jesus

But here is the key truth that I find in this story: this passage speaks to us of Jesus. I see here a picture of our Lord Jesus himself. This is a type ... a figure ... a pattern ... of the Savior.

Years and years ago, an evangelist visited our church. He was also an accomplished violinist who left the Toronto Symphony to play for the Lord. He was a meticulous and thorough Bible scholar, and I still remember what that Canadian saint of God, Arthur E. Smith, told me (a young pastor at that time): "You never know the full meaning, or the complete interpretation, of any passage of scripture until you see some references to Jesus.

"And," he continued, "No matter where you read, you can find Jesus on every page of this holy book."

I've discovered that he was right. From the first chapter of Genesis to the final chapter of Revelation, the footsteps of Jesus are evident — sometimes prominent; other times, hidden ... sometimes obvious; other times, veiled ... sometimes unmistakable; other times, shadowy. He walks on every page of the Holy Word.

Take a look at this story. Here are three phrases which summarize the whole passage:

1. The gift of the son
2. The death of the son
3. The raising of the son.

Immediately you see the parallel with Jesus:

1. The gift of the son — the gift of our Father's unfailing grace. — "Unto us a child is born, unto us a son is given (Isaiah 9:6)." "For God so loved the world that he gave his only begotten Son (John 3:16)." "Thanks be unto God for his unspeakable gift (2 Corinthians 9:15)."

75

2. The death of the son — in our behalf. — "The Son of Man is come, not to be ministered unto, but to minister, and to give his life, a ransom for many (Matthew 20:28)." "I am the good shepherd; the good shepherd giveth his life for the sheep (John 10:11)." "I lay down my life for the sheep . . . no man taketh it from me, but I lay it down of myself (John 10:15, 18)." "Greater love hath no man than this, that a man lay down his life for his friends. Ye are my friends, if ye do whatsoever I command you (John 15:13, 14)." "Christ died for our sins (1 Corinthians 15:3)." "All we like sheep have gone astray . . . and the Lord hath laid on him the iniquity of us all (Isaiah 53:6)."

He was wounded — for us. He was bruised — for us. He died — for us. Ah, yes, but that was not the end.

3. The raising of the son — to assure us of our own eternal life. "Because I live, you shall live also (John 14:19)." "The wages of sin is death, but the gift of God is eternal life, through Jesus Christ our Lord (Romans 6:23)." "God so loved the world that he gave his only begotten Son, that whosoever believeth in him should not perish, but have everlasting life (John 3:16)." "I am the resurrection and the life; he that believeth in me, though he were dead, yet shall he live (John 11:25)."

This is the assurance . . . the promise . . . the hope . . . the guarantee . . . that Almighty God has sealed upon our future: we have, for all of eternity:

       1. the gift of the Son
       2. the death of the Son
       3. the raising of the Son.

A Slave Girl
Who Saved
Her Master

For personal reading: *2 Kings 5*

For public reading: *2 Kings 5:1-5*

Outline

The Bible Story

The Little Maid: Good For Evil

Naaman: Obey And Live

Q-SHEET

A Slave Girl Who Saved Her Master

2 Kings 5

Quiz: *(Match the columns. Try first without a Bible; then use the verses to verify each answer.)*

1. _____ the little maid's homeland (5:2, 4)
2. _____ the little maid's captors' homeland (5:2)
3. _____ the little maid's mistress (5:2, 3)
4. _____ the little maid's prophet (5:3)
5. _____ capital of the little maid's homeland (5:3)
6. _____ captain of the host (general) (5:1)
7. _____ sent a letter and rich gifts (5:5)
8. _____ upset and angry because of the letter (5:7)
9. _____ man of God (5:8)
10. _____ a leper (5:1)
11. _____ river in Israel (5:10, 12)
12. _____ very angry with the prophet (5:11, 12)
13. _____ river in Damascus (5:12)
14. _____ river in Damascus (5:12)
15. _____ capital of Syria (5:12)
16. _____ god of the Syrians (5:18)
17. _____ dipped seven times in a river (5:14)
18. _____ refused to accept valuable gifts (5:16)

A. Abana
B. Damascus
C. Elisha
D. Israel
E. Jordan
F. King of Israel
G. King of Syria
H. Mrs. Naaman
I. Naaman
J. Pharpar
K. Rimmon
L. Samaria
M. Syria

78

Questions: *(for individual consideration and/or group discussion)*

1. When we have been wronged, it is so natural to seek revenge. How forgiving are we expected to be? How far should we go in returning good for evil (5:1-3)?

2. What strange, unexpected, baffling requests (maybe even "demands") does God sometimes make of us (5:10)? How do we respond (5:11, 12)?

3. Leprosy and many other diseases have been controlled by medical science. What relationship do you see between modern medicine and faith-healing (5:10, 14)?

A Slave Girl
Who Saved Her Master

Once upon a time, in the northern section of the kingdom of Israel, there was a happy family — a family, a mother and several children. But they lived in constant fear because their home was so near to the land of Syria. Every once in a while, a band of soldiers would cross the border . . . sweep down into their village (and neighboring villages) . . . steal everything they could find . . . carry it back to Syria . . . sell it . . . and make extra money for themselves.

One day a band of Syrian soldiers made an excursion into Israel . . . raided that particular village . . . stormed into that home . . . and stole a little girl. We would call it kidnapping today. They just took the little girl away from her home . . . away from her village . . . away from her homeland . . . away from her parents, her family, her friends and her playmates. And they carried her back into the land of Syria.

There she was sold — just like all the other goods and possessions that these soldiers had plundered. She was sold as a slave to one of the chief officers of the Syrian army, a man named Naaman. He bought the little girl, took her home and presented her to his wife, "Here is a new servant for you."

Children, imagine how your parents would feel if you were stolen from the family. They wouldn't be very happy about it.

Now imagine how you would feel if you were kidnapped . . . taken into a foreign country . . . and sold as a slave. You wouldn't be very happy about it, either. It would be a terrifying experience.

This little maid must have been a brave little girl. To have endured such a horrible ordeal, such a frightening nightmare, would have really taken much strength . . . courage . . . and spunk.

But she did find herself in a nice home, where General Naaman and his wife were kind to her. Naaman was a rich man, with a large house . . . numerous servants . . . considerable possessions. He was a prominent and influential man — a very close friend of the king. Indeed, when the king went into the temple to worship, he would often take Naaman, his loyal companion, with him.

The people who lived in Syria did not know about the one true God. They were a heathen people. They were religious — but they worshipped an idol, an idol named Rimmon. They built great temples, and in those temples they had large statues — idols — of their god, Rimmon. They would bow themselves before those idols and would offer their prayers and their gifts to them.

Yes, Naaman was rich and powerful and prominent — but there was one thing that was wrong with him: he was a sick man. Naaman had — leprosy. Even though it has been pretty well conquered today, leprosy is still a dreadful disease. When it begins, the skin starts to turn white — in little patches in different places — usually on the hands, sometimes on the face and sometimes on the feet. Then these patches slowly become bigger and bigger ... begin to hurt ... and finally reach the place where the fingers and the hands become useless. In the days of the Bible, it was a dreadful, repulsive, menacing, incurable disease. And though he was wealthy and powerful, General Naaman had leprosy.

The brave little maid, the slave girl from Israel, soon adjusted and made herself at home (as best she could) as an attendant for Mrs. Naaman. Before long, she realized what was wrong with her master, and one day she remarked to her mistress, "I only wish the general could go back down into Israel, where I came from. Down there, there's a man of God, a prophet ... and he could heal the general; he could cure him of his leprosy. I know he could."

The little girl's statement reached Naaman — and the king, because Naaman was the king's closest friend. And the king of Syria declared, "Well, now, we'll find out about this. I'll write a letter to the king of Israel, and command him to heal my general."

And so he wrote the letter ... gathered together many valuable gifts (silver, gold, beautiful clothing) ... and sent Naaman, with his many servants and guards, down into Israel.

When Naaman and his caravan arrived in the city of Samaria (the capital of Israel at that time, and the residence of the king), they went at once to the palace and delivered the letter from the king of Syria.

The king of Israel read the letter — and thundered, "Who does he think I am? God? How can I heal leprosy? He's just using this as an excuse to start another war." The king didn't know what to do or say — he worried ... fussed ... fretted.

Meanwhile, Naaman was waiting for an answer, wondering, "What's going on here? Why is he taking so long? Maybe he's sending for the man of God and will bring him here, to the palace."

But while the king of Israel was grumbling and brooding, another message came for him. This time it was from the prophet Elisha, and stated, "I understand your problem. But why do you worry? Send the man to me, and he will know that there is a god in Israel."

We aren't sure why the king didn't seem to know about Elisha. The main reason, probably was that he didn't care much about holy matters; he was not a godly king and didn't really know the true God.

But the king was delighted to find an answer to his predicament and instructed Naaman, "You'll need to go to the house of a certain man," and guided him to the home of Elisha, the man of God.

When Naaman arrived, Elisha didn't even go out to meet him, but sent a servant, who said to General Naaman, "My master tells you to go down to the river Jordan and dip yourself in the water seven times."

Imagine Naaman ... putting his hands on his hips ... analyzing the situation ... and thinking to himself (and probably even expressing it aloud), "What is going on here? Who is this fellow? Here I am, the man close to the king, and I come to ask for his help. I bring him these presents, and he doesn't even come out to say hello. He sends out a servant. There's something wrong with this man.

"And dip in the river Jordan? If dipping in the water would make any difference, I'd go back home — we have better water there, in Damascus. We have the river Abana there. Why should I bathe in the muddy old Jordan?"

And Naaman was angry. Naaman was furious. The Bible says he was "wroth" and "went away in a rage." He was ready to start back home.

But some of Naaman's company realized that there was more to Elisha's prescription than simply dipping in the river. So one of his captains came to him and pleaded, "Look, if the prophet told you to do some great, strange thing, you would do it. If he told you to give him more gold or more horses, you would do it. If he told you to get down on your hands and knees and crawl home to Syria and you would certainly be healed, you would do it."

The Bible doesn't say all that. It just says that the officer urged Naaman to obey Elisha, "What he asks you to do is a simple thing. Why don't you do it? We've come all this distance. It can't hurt to try."

And, thank the Lord, Naaman was sensible enough, even in his anger, to understand that the officer spoke the truth.

So down he went to the banks of the Jordan River . . . waded in . . . dipped himself . . . and came up.

His skin hadn't changed. He dipped the second time. No difference. Three times . . . four . . . five . . . six. Still no change.

Then the seventh dip — and when he stood up, his flesh was like a baby's: clean . . . soft . . . pure . . . fresh . . . healed!

Naaman was excited! He had almost missed it! Imagine him running swiftly back to the prophet's home. Picture him offering all of the gifts: "Here is the silver! Here is the gold! Here are the beautiful robes and fabrics! Take them — all of them! And if you want more, I'll get it!"

But Elisha said, "No," refusing the gifts — even though Naaman beseeched him to accept. Elisha was demonstrating that there are some values ... some truths about God ... that cannot be bought.

Naaman and his caravan returned to Syria — and I keep wondering what happened when he got home. The Bible doesn't tell us. But I wonder how he treated the little Hebrew girl. I wonder how he said, "thank you" to her. We don't know. I like to think that he made arrangements for her to return to her parents in Israel. But we don't know. We don't even know the little girl's name. That's a shame, isn't it? Because that unknown little girl was the instrument for the healing of the general of the Syrian army.

The Little Maid: Good For Evil

This Hebrew maid told her master and her mistress about God ... the living God ... the true God. There she was — in strange circumstances, in a life that was difficult and lonely. But she did the best she could; she made the most of what she had. She tried to be pleasant ... contented ... diligent ... cheerful ... industrious ... useful. And she remembered what she had learned from her mother and father — and from her pastor. She had been taught about God — and she had no hesitation about telling her master and her mistress. She shared what she knew, what she believed.

When she discovered that her master, the general, was a very sick man, she could have said, "Well, good for him. He deserves it. That's what ought to happen to these Syrians, these pagans. I wish they all had leprosy."

She might have said that — but she didn't. She could not find it in her heart to be happy because somebody else was sad ... to rejoice because somebody else faced tragedy and heartache ... to return hate for hate, evil for evil.

Instead she tried to share her knowledge, her understanding of God. We do not know how she knew of Elisha. We

84

do not know whether she had ever met Elisha. But somehow she had learned about the prophet, the man of God . . . believed in his miraculous powers . . . and was willing, even eager, to talk about him to others who needed supernatural help.

In many ways, this little maid was a Christian hundreds of years before Jesus was born. In a very real sense, this is true. She was a little girl who turned the other cheek (Matthew 6:39) . . . who overcame evil with good (Romans 12:21) . . . who did whatever she could to help people — even those who had kidnapped her.

Naaman: Obey And Live

In Naaman, the general, we see a picture of many people today — a type of an unsaved person seeking for salvation, of a heathen finding his way to the true God. Let us, in a rapid review, trace the steps.

1. Naaman was a great man . . . a wealthy man . . . an influential man . . . a strong brave man. He was honored; he enjoyed luxury and riches, power and prestige. It is a fact that a heathen may possess many material and worldly advantages. It is possible for heathens, for those who don't know the true God, to secure earthly privileges and prosperity.

We usually think of a heathen as a savage, uncivilized, primitive barbarian — but a heathen may be a nice person, a rich person, an influential person, or even a royal person. Someone could have all of these qualities — and still not know God.

A person may be decent . . . respected . . . cultured . . . educated . . . successful . . . intelligent . . . and be a pagan. A person may be kind . . . considerate . . . benevolent . . . generous . . . humanitarian . . . and be a heathen.

2. Naaman suffered from a deadly disease. As great as he was, as rich as he was, not one slave in the entire land of Syria would have traded skin with him. He was sick — afflicted with leprosy.

And leprosy, throughout the Bible, is a type, or picture, of sin. As leprosy eats away at the body of a person, so sin eats away at the soul — bringing decay and destruction.

Today, as in the Bible days, there are many who delight in their prosperous abundance ... who are great in the eyes of the world ... but who are doomed with a dreadful disease — sin.

3. Naaman heard about a possible cure, through an insignificant agency — a little servant girl, a Hebrew maid who had been captured on one of their raids and brought back to Syria.

Who would have ever suspected that such a little girl could awaken the possibility of healing?

And who would suspect that some of the little things that we do, or say, could start somebody on the pathway to salvation? This little slave girl, with her simple faith, started Naaman toward God. So it may be that, without realizing it, a believer ... a missionary ... an evangelist ... a pastor ... a Sunday school teacher ... a mother ... a father ... a neighbor — can say, or do just the right thing at the right time to start someone in the right direction.

You aren't always aware of how much influence you might have. You can hand somebody a tract — just a small leaflet that tells about Jesus.

You can write "God bless you" in a letter. Or "God loves you, and I love you too." And you may never know what that means to the one who reads that letter.

The little things that we do are important. A little incident can leave a large impression.

Naaman, with all of his material advantages, afflicted with leprosy, heard about a possible cure — through the quiet witness of a Jewish slave girl.

4. Naaman wanted to be healed. He started off to seek diligently the means of deliverance — and was willing to pay the price: no cost was too demanding ... no toil too strenuous ... no journey too long ... no sacrifice too costly. He sought — earnestly. He searched fervently. And he found the man of God.

5. Naaman (like many modern heathens) was offended at the remedy that was prescribed for his cure — and resisted. He came to the doctor; the doctor wrote a prescription; and Naaman was ready to tear it up and throw it in the trash can.

In today's world, this is still true — literally. You go to the doctor — you pay him good money. He tells you what to do — and you pay no attention to him.

You go to church. The Lord tells you what to do — and you pay no attention to him.

Naaman said, "I surely expected that the prophet himself would meet me and welcome me. After all, I'm an important, distinguished man — next to the king. Look at all these chariots, all these servants, all these soldiers, all this retinue that I have with me. I thought he'd certainly greet me."

And Naaman continued to rebuke Elisha, "I thought he would probably make some mysterious signs or motions . . . concoct a magical potion . . . or pronounce his secret incantations."

There are still those with their own pre-conceived ideas as to how salvation will be achieved. They already have in their mind the way they expect deliverance to come — and anything different will confuse and upset them. And they are offended at the story of the cross.

Naaman was irritated and enraged at the simplicity of what Elisha told him to do: "Go and dip seven times in the river Jordan."

A child can understand that — anybody can understand that. A child can do it — anybody can do it. It's so simple. But it made Naaman angry.

So it is with the plan of salvation — it is amazingly simple. God says, "Just repent — and believe in my Son . . . he died for you . . . your sins are forgiven . . . only trust him."

A child can understand that — anybody can understand that. A child can do it — anybody can do it. It's so simple — God designed it that way. There is nothing complex or complicated about it.

Why become enraged at the preacher . . . at the church . . . at the Bible . . . when they proclaim the simple message of the healing power in the cross of Jesus?

If such anger would cure your leprosy, your sin, that would be marvelous. But all the anger in the world will not save you. Indignation is no substitute for obedience. God's method is so simple.

6. Naaman was cured. When he finally was obedient, he was healed. "Just dip seven times," Naaman was told. And when he came up the seventh time, his skin was cleansed and purified — the leprosy had disappeared! Not the water (neither of the Jordan in Israel nor of the Abana in Syria) cured Naaman — it was his obedience.

If you were seeking salvation today, and God told you to do "some great thing," you would do it — if at all possible. If God said, "Establish a memorial," you would try. If God said, "Give $25,000 to your church," you would scrounge around and raise $25,000 — somehow. If God said, "Take a trip to the Holy Land, and dip yourself seven times in the river Jordan," you would manage to do it.

But you don't need to establish a memorial ... raise $25,000 ... go to the Holy Land ... or bathe in the river Jordan.

All you need to do is lift up your eyes to the cross of Jesus. That is God's way — it is so simple, so easy. All he asks is repentance ... trust ... obedience. Sometimes we may think God's way seems silly or foolish. But obey. Just obey — and live.

Part III — Some New Testament Children

A Boy Who Was Lost On A Holiday

For personal reading: *Luke 2:41-52*

For public reading: *Luke 2:41-52*

Outline

The Bible Story

Some Observations

The Day Of Absorption

The Day Of Concern

The Day Of Discovery

89

A Boy Who Was Lost On A Holiday
Luke 2:41-52

Quiz: *(Fill in the blanks. Try first without a Bible; then use the verses to verify each answer.)*

1-3. Jesus was _____ years old when his parents took him to the city of _____ for the feast of the _____ (2:41, 42).

4, 5. When the caravan started home to the town of _____, Jesus stayed in the city of _____ (2:39, 43, 51).

6. He was not missed until the group had traveled _____ (2:44).

7-9. Jesus was separated from his parents for _____ days before he was found in the _____, sitting among the learned _____ (2:46).

10, 11. His reply to his _____ was, "Wist ye not that I must be about my Father's _____ (2:48, 49)?"

12. Jesus returned to the village of _____ (2:51).

13-16. "Jesus increased in _____ and _____, and in favor with _____ and _____ (2:52)."

Questions: *(for individual consideration and/or group discussion)*

1. When, in your opinion, did Jesus know he was the Messiah, the Son of God (2:49)? From a baby? In the temple? At his baptism (see Mark 1:9-11)? At the transfiguration (see Mark 9:11ff)? In Gethsemane (see Mark 14:32ff)? Did he know it all the time? Or did he learn it? Suddenly or gradually?

2. How closely should we supervise the children in our care (2:43, 44)? Should we know exactly where they are at all times? Can parents be overly protective? What, if any, are the values of a curfew?

3. What examples can you give of well-rounded persons (2:52)? Or of one-sided ones? Does our society promote full and complete development of the personality when our athletes, actors/actresses, musicians, entertainers, receive such distorted compensation? Should this be changed? Can it be changed? How?

A Boy Who Was
Lost On A Holiday

A long time ago, there was a small-town family that journeyed into the big city for a holiday. It was an extra-special and wonderful time for the 12-year-old boy of the family, who was deeply impressed with the large, beautiful church — famous all over the country.

The family traveled with a number of friendly, neighboring families from their home town. When the vacation period was over, they all left the city and started back home. That first evening, the husband and wife got together — after spending the day in different groups.

But where was their 12-year-old boy? Neither of them knew! Each parent had thought he was with the other — or with some of his village playmates. Frantically, they searched among all their friends. But nobody could help — nobody had seen the boy. He was gone ... missing ... lost!

The following morning (after a fearful, sleepless night) the worried parents headed back toward the city. There they searched diligently, their hearts filled with anxiety and apprehension. Then finally — they found him! Where? In the magnificent church that had so impressed the lad!

Does the story begin to sound familiar? Yes, of course. It's the story of Jesus! He was the 12-year-old boy and the parents were Mary and Joseph.

The well-known story is of a trip to the city of Jerusalem to celebrate the feast of Passover. For weeks, Jesus had been making plans for the trip, eagerly looking forward to visiting the holy city. He could hardly wait! It was so exciting! A dream was coming true!

Finally, the time came. Jesus and his parents traveled with a number of other families from Nazareth, their home town. There were aunts and uncles ... nephews and nieces ... cousins and playmates ... friends and neighbors. They formed a caravan: traveling together ... eating together ... camping together. (It was like a traveling reunion or a traveling picnic.) In Bible times, it was a long trip to Jerusalem — at least three days, and probably more.

When the company arrived in the holy city, Jesus was overwhelmed with all the new and different sights to see ... places to go ... things to do. There were tall buildings ... bustling marketplaces ... noisy crowds ... colorful robes and uniforms ... surging traffic ... busy bazaars. All of this (and much more) captured the intense interest of the excited young boy.

But with all these attractions clamoring for his attention, Jesus quickly centered his interest in one place — the holy temple — with its towering pillars ... marble colonnades ... marvelous courts. There the sacrifices were offered ... the rituals and ceremonies were performed ... the Law and the Prophets were taught. There — everywhere evident — were the priests ... the scholars ... the rabbis ... the Pharisees ... the Roman soldiers ... the temple police.

Jesus had looked forward to this. It was everything he had expected — and more! He was captivated ... fascinated ... engrossed! So much so that he forgot completely about his parents ... the caravan ... the return to Nazareth ... or anything else. For him — time stood still.

Meanwhile, the caravan of families had started back to Nazareth — and Jesus was unwittingly left behind in Jerusalem. Mary and Joseph each assumed he was with the other — or with some of his village friends. Not until the first evening, when the families made camp for overnight, was it discovered that the boy Jesus was nowhere to be found.

Very early the next morning, after a long, sleepless night of suspense, Mary and Joseph left for Jerusalem — looking for him all the way. How worried they must have been.

They hunted everywhere. At length, they found him — now, how relieved they must have been. You don't need to guess where, do you? He was in the temple, in the impressive church, sitting with the doctors and teachers of the Law, eagerly absorbing all the knowledge he could, taking advantage of this great opportunity to expand his horizons.

The story closes as Jesus returned with Mary and Joseph to their home in Nazareth, where he remained for the next 18 years (see Luke 3:23).

Some Observations

This incident provides the only glimpse of Jesus we have between his birth and the beginning of his public ministry. Of the years after his birth and the flight to Egypt (Matthew 2:13-23), the Bible tells us nothing about the boyhood of Jesus.

Then this visit to Jerusalem at age 12 is recorded, after which we once more have a period of silence for 18 years.

How we would like to know more — about his childhood and youth ... about his daily life as a growing boy ... about the games he played ... the fun he enjoyed ... his work as a carpenter ... his activities until age 30. But God, in his infinite wisdom, has chosen not to reveal this to us.

———

There is nothing in this story to indicate any neglect or carelessness on the part of Mary or Joseph. It was a common practice for several families to travel together — and these families were so well-acquainted that the children of one family were the children of another.

That isn't unusual. It still happens today — your mothers know what it's like to have your playmate come in for a drink of water ... for a cookie ... to use the phone ... or the bathroom. Your friend doesn't really belong to your family — and yet, seems a part of it. That's the situation we had here — Mary and Joseph took it for granted that Jesus was in the caravan, and that people who cared were looking after him.

And it is no surprise that Mary and Joseph were separated for most of the day. It was normal for the women — and the men — to travel separately. Indeed, in a caravan like this, the women often started off earlier than the men — since they traveled more slowly. Then, the men would start later — and move faster. And the two groups might not join until they pitched camp in the evening.

We do learn something here, by inference, about the home life of Jesus in Nazareth ... about the kind of parents Mary and Joseph were ... about the qualities that Jesus was developing.

It is easy to note that Jesus — was spiritually perceptive ("They found him in the temple") ... had a keen mind and was teachable (he was eager to learn, "sitting in the midst of the doctors") ... was obedient (he was "subject unto them").

Such qualities are developed in the family — so it seems certain that the home life at Nazareth cultivated wisdom, understanding ... faith and insight ... discipline and respect.

Another element in the atmosphere of that home life must have been love. What a genuine tribute to Joseph that Jesus used the word "Father" to describe the highest and the holiest that he knew!

As this incident closes, we are told that Jesus possessed a well-rounded personality. He was neither an abnormal genius nor a precocious fanatic. As he grew, he increased in wisdom (mentally — he was intelligent) and stature (physically — he was strong) and in favor with God (spiritually — he was devout) and in favor with man (socially — he was popular).

Would that each of us, like Jesus, should develop in such a well-rounded manner!

The Day Of Absorption

A summary of this story could be expressed in the phrase, "three days without Jesus:"

Day 1 — from the city of Jerusalem to the encampment for the night — probably somewhere between Bethel and

95

Sychar. There Mary and Joseph realized that they were without Jesus.

Day 2 — from the overnight stop back to Jerusalem. That was another day without Jesus.

Day 3 — they hunted in the city — until they found their boy.

Three days without Jesus: We find here a parable of our own Christian experience. Many of us, in varying degrees, have followed a similar pattern.

The first day was the Day of Absorption — they were so absorbed with what they were doing and with all that had happened in Jerusalem that they never knew that Jesus was missing. A whole day went by — and they never realized that he wasn't there.

What they were doing wasn't wrong ... wicked ... or evil. They just don't notice that Jesus wasn't around.

Isn't that an accurate portrayal of the way that many of us live? How often have you gone a whole day without Jesus — and didn't realize at all that Jesus was missing? What you were doing may not have been sinful — but remember the picture that Jesus painted when he illustrated indifference and neglect; he said:

> "As it was in the days of Noah, so shall it be also in the days of the Son of man. They did eat, they drank, they married wives, they were given in marriage, until the day that Noah entered into the ark, and the flood came, and destroyed them all. Likewise also, as it was in the days of Lot; they did eat, they drank, they bought, they sold, they planted, they builded; But the same day that Lot went out of Sodom, it rained fire and brimstone from heaven, and destroyed them all. Even thus shall it be in the days when the Son of man is revealed (Luke 17:26-30)."

Jesus was talking about the last days and the wickedness that would precede them. He compared that time with the times of Noah and of Lot.

What was it like in the days of Noah? We consider it as a very wicked time — so wicked that God sent a flood, in judgment.

How did Jesus describe it? "They did eat, they drank, they married wives, they were given in marriage, until . . . the flood came and destroyed them all."

And what was it like in the days of Lot (another period of great evil and degradation)? How did Jesus describe it? "They did eat, they drank, they bought, they sold, they planted, they builded, but . . . it rained fire and brimstone . . . and destroyed them all."

Jesus didn't say, "As it was in the days of Noah, when men were wicked . . . drunkards . . . thieves . . . murderers . . . addicts . . . reprobates."

No, he didn't say that. He simply said, "In the days of Noah, and of Lot — when people went about the normal, ordinary, routine business of every-day living, and neglected the Lord completely, never even thinking about him."

Eating and drinking . . . buying and selling . . . building and planting . . . marrying and raising families — these are not wrong. They're perfectly legitimate, all of them until they take the place of God, until they consume so much of our time and energy that we never even notice that the Lord isn't around.

Enjoying pleasure . . . making a living . . . providing comforts . . . seeking security . . . appreciating home life: these activities are not immoral or sinful; they are not wrong — except they are never to become first.

"Seek ye first the kingdom of God and his righteousness . . . (Matthew 6:33)."

"Thou shalt have no other gods before me (Exodus 20:3)." That's the Day of Absorption — being so preoccupied with the affairs of every-day living that we are not even aware that Jesus isn't with us.

The Day Of Concern

The second day without Jesus is the Day of Concern. We can imagine the emotions of Mary and Joseph during that

97

night; we can be sure they didn't get much sleep. And very early in the morning, they were off, heading back to Jerusalem, wondering all the way what had happened. They were concerned ... anxious ... frightened.

This is true of us — when we realize that Jesus is missing, there's a certain amount of fear and anxiety. We recognize our spiritual emptiness; we are waked up; we become concerned, so concerned that we determine to do something about it.

But how often we try to satisfy our fears in wrong ways. We go seeking after false religions ... sects ... cults. And all they do is tell us how to try to save ourselves — how to pull ourselves up by our own bootstraps.

A crucial factor in determining the validity of any religion is whether it is auto-soteric. What does this mean? Auto-matic means self-working. Auto-mobile means self-moving. Autograph means self-writing. Auto-soteric means self-saving. And the heart of the Christian gospel is that we cannot — in any way or by any means — save ourselves.

At the core of false religions, the emphasis is on what we do — not what Jesus does. And we are not saved by what we do — we are saved by what Jesus has done for us. Remember this. He is the one who is central and supreme. We are not delivered by ourselves, but from ourselves — by Jesus, the Savior.

The rich young ruler came to Jesus, and asked, "What shall I do to inherit eternal life (see Luke 18:18ff)?"

This is the question of the ages. Everybody wants to know, "What can I do?" We want to earn or deserve forgiveness ... salvation ... eternal life ... justification ... righteousness.

What do you need to do? Nothing! It's done for you. You simply believe — and accept. It's an act of faith for us. It's an act of grace — for God.

The Day Of Discovery

The third day, then, is the Day of Discovery — the day we find Jesus. That's a great day!

Mary and Joseph returned to Jerusalem. There they found Jesus, and — of all places — they found him in the church.

You want to find Jesus? You realize that he is missing; you are concerned that he is missing. You want to find him? Where do you go? To church. That's where they went. That's where they found him.

They searched other places, and Jesus was surprised. "How is it," he said, in his first recorded words, "How is it that you went other places to look for me? Didn't you know that I must be about my Father's business? You should have expected to find me here." (He didn't say it exactly that way — but the implication is there.)

When you want a haircut, you don't go to a dentist. When you want medical attention, you don't go to a mechanic. When you want legal advice, you don't go to a nurse. Some people are trained to do certain things. When you want to find Jesus, where should you go? To those who know him, love him, serve him, and are trained to help you find him.

Now notice: when Jesus was found in church, he was not with the crowds. He was with the leaders, the spiritual people — those who were searching their scriptures, seeking eternal truths.

We can criticize the scribes and Pharisees all we want — later in his life, Jesus criticized them very harshly (see Matthew 23) because they became self-righteous, hypocritical and rigidly formal. But they were the dedicated leaders ... those trying to obey the Law ... the ones searching for the way of holiness. And Jesus was with them.

There may be some people in your church ... in any city ... all over the world ... who are not there for spiritual purposes. They come for other reasons — they are part of the crowd.

But there are also those who know Jesus, and who can lead you to him. Seek them out.

The day we discover Jesus is a great day, a day of joy ... emotion ... blessing ... cleansing ... excitement!

The day we discover Jesus, brings life ... new life ... abundant life ... eternal life!

The day we discover Jesus, we experience transforming love ... redeeming grace ... dynamic power ... divine guidance ... soothing comfort!

The day we discover Jesus is beyond description; it is incredible ... overwhelming ... life-changing ... triumphant!

Every person can experience this Day of Discovery. Find Jesus today and thrill at the glory of knowing him, loving him and walking with him.

And if you have already discovered Jesus, may today be the time for you to remember and renew this tremendous experience.

A Boy
Who Gave Away
His Lunch

For personal reading:
Matthew 14:13-21
Mark 6:30-44
Luke 9:10-17
John 6:1-14

For public reading:
John 6:1-14

Outline

The Bible Story

Be Like Jesus

Be Like Andrew

Be Like The Boy

Q-SHEET

A Boy Who Gave Away His Lunch
Luke 6:1-14

Quiz: *(Circle the correct word. Try first without a Bible; then use the verses to verify each answer.)*

1-3. The boy carried a (lunch, cooler, net) which contained five (wheat, unleavened, barley) loaves and two small (toys, frogs, fish) (6:9).

4-7. He went to a (park, mountain, kibbutz) near the (Mediterranean Sea, Sea of Galilee, Jordan River) and the time of the (Passover, Pentecost, Pentateuch), a Jewish (commandment, feast, creed), was at hand (6:1-4).

8, 9. He was part of a crowd where the (men, women, children) numbered about (50, 500, 5,000) (6:10).

10-12. He became acquainted with (Philip, Andrew, Joseph), a (brother, cousin, neighbor) of (Peter, Zebedee, Nicodemus) (6:8, 9).

13-16. He gave his (lunch, cooler, net) to Jesus, who said a (benediction, poem, blessing) and gave it to (Tiberias, Philip, the disciples), who in turn gave it to (Andrew, the people, the disciples) (6:11).

17-18. When the crowd had (cheered, eaten, dispersed), twelve (barrels, bushels, baskets) of fragments were gathered (6:12, 13).

Questions: *(for individual consideration and/or group discussion)*

1. This miracle is the only miracle of Jesus which is recorded in all four of the gospel accounts (Matthew 14:13-21; Mark 6:30-44; Luke 9:10-17; John 6:1-14). What significance, if any, do you find in this?

2. If Jesus felt the need for rest and quiet, prayer and meditation, why do we sometimes think we can do without it (Mark 6:31, 32, 46; see also Mark 1:35; Luke 5:16; 6:12; 9:28)?

3. What reaction do you have when someone intrudes on your privacy? How does it compare with the response of Jesus (Mark 6:33, 34)?

4. How can this miracle be reconciled with the Temptation experience of Jesus, when he refused to turn stones into bread (Matthew 4:1-4)?

A Boy Who
Gave Away His Lunch

In the days of the Bible, there once lived a boy and his mother, near the Sea of Galilee. He was a typical boy: active . . . inquisitive . . . energetic . . . open to ideas . . . explorative.

One sunny spring morning, near the time of the Passover, he asked his mother for permission to take a long hike — to the other side of the village of Bethsaida. For several days, he had heard some of the neighbors talking about an unusual man . . . a miracle worker . . . a healer . . . a magician. And just the day before, the boy had learned from the village stonecutter that this great man was close at hand, in their own area.

"And," added the boy to his mother, "I really want to see him, while he is so near. His name is Jesus. He is from Nazareth . . . and all the men say that he is someone special — some of them even think he may be the Messiah. Please, Mother, let me go. I may never have another chance like this."

What mother could resist such pleading? And so the boy was on his way, after promising to be careful and sensible — and also after his mother had quickly prepared a small lunch for him to carry: five little barley loaves and two tiny fish. They were a poor family and barley was the cheapest grain. It wasn't very much, but the mother knew that her son would get hungry during the day — and this snack would help to satisfy him.

As he skipped along, the lad gradually became more and more aware of more and more people. He had expected a lonely walk and he had thought that he might have some difficulty in finding this man Jesus.

But it was not so. He was not alone — and he had no problem finding Jesus. He just moved along with the people. Everybody seemed to be going in the same direction — to the same place. The numbers increased — until by the time he reached the place where Jesus was, the crowds were up into the hundreds — even thousands — spread all over the grassy hillside, overlooking the Sea of Galilee. The boy was dumb-founded, overwhelmed.

And he was also overwhelmed by the stories that Jesus told and the truths that Jesus taught. This Jesus was a magnetic person — a powerful preacher. Just think, there he was — speaking out in the open . . . to a crowd of thousands . . . with no loud speakers . . . and yet no one had any trouble hearing him! And it seemed to the boy (and to each listener) that Jesus was talking to him, personally — not to a vast crowd. The boy was completely fascinated.

There were intermissions in the preaching — because even a man as strong as Jesus could not continue to speak all day long. So he would preach for a while, and then there would be a break. While Jesus would try to rest a bit, his disciples circulated among the crowds to meet individual needs.

During one of these interludes, the lad was approached by one of the disciples — a friendly fisherman, named Andrew, who struck up an acquaintance with the boy, enjoyed the conversation, and took a personal interest in him.

They discussed many interesting topics: fishing . . . tying knots . . . boats . . . the kind of bait to use . . . how to cast a net . . . where and when to find certain kinds of fish in the lake.

But Andrew was also a fisher of men — and talked to the boy about Jesus . . . the Master . . . the Messiah . . . the Savior. And finally, late in the afternoon — he brought the boy to Jesus. He wanted the lad to meet Jesus personally.

As the two of them drew near to Jesus, they heard him talking with Philip (another disciple) about how to feed all these people. The day was drawing to a close . . . the crowd was tired and weary . . . everyone was getting hungry. "How can we feed them?" Jesus was asking.

Then the boy heard Philip reply, "We can't. We haven't any food here. And even if we had money, we couldn't buy enough. There isn't any place in this whole area where we can buy food for this many people. We must send them away to their homes — each to go in his own direction, and to care for his own needs."

At that point, Andrew interrupted ... introduced the young boy to Jesus ... and remarked, "Here is a lad who has a lunch — five barley loaves and two fish."

Then he thought how silly this sounded, and quickly added, "But of course, what are they among a crowd like this?"

But the boy was willing to give his lunch to Jesus — and said so, before Jesus had time to respond to Andrew.

Immediately, Jesus took charge. "Organize the crowd," he instructed the disciples, "Separate them into groups — of fifties and hundreds."

When this was done, he took the lunch ... bowed his head ... blessed the food ... then broke the loaves and the fish. "Here, distribute these," he said, as he handed the food to his followers.

What happened was incredible! The boy couldn't believe what he saw. He watched in awe as Andrew and Philip (and the other disciples) moved out to pass the food to the people. Each disciple had a small piece of bread, and as he broke it and handed it to the people in the rows — there was always more to break off! It was like the oil in the cruse, back in the days of Elijah and Elisha (1 Kings 17:8-16; 2 Kings 4:1-6) — it never ran out! The bread never came to an end — there was always another piece to break!

The boy's eyes opened wide — with amazement ... fascination ... wonder ... incredulity ... astonishment! What he saw was unbelievable! Yet he himself had witnessed it. He was there. He saw it. All over his face was written an indelible expression of bewilderment and surprise! He watched his five barley loaves and two fish feed more than 5,000 people! He was literally spellbound ... transfixed ... dazzled!

What an exciting story he had to tell his mother that night when he returned home!

Be Like Jesus

In this tremendous incident, we have met three principal characters: the boy with the lunch ... Andrew, the disciple

106

... and Jesus, the Lord. Each sets an example for us to follow; each demonstrates a quality for us to develop.

There are obviously many ways in which Jesus sets an example for us. He was human, and overcame the same temptations and obstacles that we face. We who are his disciples today desire to do our utmost to be like our Master. James Rowe expressed it well in his gospel song:

> *"Earthly pleasures vainly call me;*
> *I would be like Jesus;*
> *Nothing worldly shall enthrall me;*
> *I would be like Jesus.*
> *Be like Jesus, this my song,*
> *In the home and in the throng;*
> *Be like Jesus, all day long!*
> *I would be like Jesus."*

The one characteristic of Jesus which is emphasized here is his deep concern for people. He needed quiet and peace — rest for the body and strength for the soul (as we all do at times). He tried to withdraw from the demanding, insistent crowds. He sought a place where he could be alone with his disciples — and with his heavenly Father. They even boarded a boat and sailed toward a secluded area.

But it was easy for the people to see where the boat was headed — and they moved faster on shore than the sailboat on the water. Jesus wanted calm and quiet — but found a clamoring crowd (Matthew 14:13, 14; Mark 6:30-34).

Jesus could have been annoyed ... resented the intrusion into his privacy ... found the throng to be a nuisance. Most of us would have reacted that way.

But not Jesus. He was "moved with compassion" (a phrase that is used very frequently to describe Jesus). We are told that he "received" them (Luke 9:11). The original Greek word could be translated "welcomed" — and is so translated in many modern versions. Think of it! He had every reason to be disturbed with the people — but recognizing their needs, he "welcomed" them.

So it was, also, when they needed food. Others (like Philip) said, "Send them away — let somebody else worry about them."

But by his actions, Jesus suggested, "We must do something — we must worry about our brothers' needs." The needs of human beings was a top priority for Jesus.

———

In essence, we can say that Jesus was a very caring person — one who was always concerned about the welfare of others. Really, he was a "care-full" person. That's what the word "careful" actually means — "full of care." (In the same way, the word "awful" literally means "full of awe." How often, in ordinary conversation, we misuse this word!)

Follow the example of Jesus — be a thoughtful, considerate, unselfish, "care-full" human being.

Be Like Andrew

Andrew was a fisherman who became a disciple of John, the Baptist . . . witnessed the baptism of Jesus . . . was stirred by John's announcement to "Behold the Lamb of God (John 1:29, 36)" . . . and became convinced that Jesus was indeed the Messiah.

We do not read much about Andrew in the New Testament, but almost every time we see him, he is busy doing what he knew how to do, doing what he did best — bringing people to Jesus.

It is no surprise that it was Andrew who found the lad with the lunch — and brought him to Jesus. That's what he was always doing. He developed a tremendous knack for bringing people to his Lord, an amazing ability to introduce people to Jesus.

———

When Andrew knew in his heart that Jesus was the Messiah ... the Christ ... the Lord ... the first thing he did was to search out his brother and bring him to Jesus (John 1:40-42).

And who was his brother? Simon, who was then given a new name by Jesus — Peter, the rock. Yes, the influential, courageous leader of the disciples — he who left a tremendous impact on the New Testament narrative — was brought to Jesus by Andrew. It is nearly impossible to imagine the history of the early church without Peter — and Andrew was the one who led Peter to Jesus.

It is never easy to bring one's own brother (or sister — or any relative) to the Savior. So Andrew has been a source of inspiration to personal workers and soul-winners ever since.

On another occasion, a group of Greeks (gentiles, outsiders) sought an audience with Jesus (John 12:20-22). They came first to Philip (probably because his name indicates a Greek background) and said, "Sir, we would see Jesus."

Philip apparently was a bit hesitant about what to do. Rather than take them to Jesus himself, he went to Andrew for advice. And it was Andrew who led the Greeks to Jesus.

Follow the example of Andrew — be a fisher of men; develop the knack of bringing people to Jesus.

Be Like The Boy

The boy who gave away his lunch demonstrates what can happen when we give all that we have to Jesus.

He did not have much — only five barley loaves and two fish — but he gave it all. And in the hands of Jesus, it multiplied ... grew ... expanded.

So it is with us. We may not have much. But we can give it away ... to Jesus ... all of it. And in his hands, it can work miracles.

We may be sorry that we have so little to offer — but that is no excuse for not giving the little that we do have.

A
Rebellious
Teenager

For personal reading: *Luke 15*

For public reading: *Luke 15:11-24*

Outline

The Bible Story

Embarrass

Embrace

Embody

Q-SHEET

A Rebellious Teenager
Luke 15

Quiz: *(Circle the correct word. Try first without a Bible; then use the verses to verify each answer.)*

1. The younger son in this story had (1, 2, 3) brothers (15:11).

2. He asked his father for (a wife, a car, an inheritance) (15:12).

3, 4. He traveled to a (luxury resort, a nearby seaport, a far country) and there he (lived happily ever after, indulged himself, became a criminal) (15:13).

5-7. When a (tornado, famine, rabbi) came, he became so (happy, healthy, hungry) that he was willing to (eat garbage, sing for joy, go to school) (15:14-16).

8, 9. He made up his mind to return to (the pigpen, the hospital, his father) and ask (for a loan, for a promotion, to be a servant) (15:17-19).

10, 11. His father ran (toward, away from, into) him and (kissed, rejected, punished) him (15:20).

12-14. He received a (haircut, reprimand, robe), a (bath, ring, banishment), and a pair of (trousers, shoes, glasses) (15:22)

15. A (lamb, calf, large hall) was prepared for a feast (15:23).

Questions: *(for individual consideration and/or group discussion)*

1. Is there any advantage (or disadvantage) in being an older (or younger) child (15:29, 30)? Why?

2. The younger son (in the pigpen) might be classified today as "homeless" (15:14-16). What is the responsibility of society for these people?

3. Is it easy (or hard) to grant forgiveness (15:20, 21)? Why? Is it easy (or hard) to accept forgiveness? Why?

A Rebellious Teenager

There once lived, in the lands of the Bible, a farmer who had two sons. The farmer was a hard worker and his land was fruitful — so he became quite wealthy.

The younger son did not like his life on the farm: it was hard work — heavy physical labor, with much exertion and sweat. It was long work — from early morning till the sun went down in the west. It was dull, boring work — with no pleasure or excitement. The young man was tired of the farm.

He was anxious to live in the city. He longed for it. He yearned for it. He dreamed about it. He desperately desired it. He wanted glamor, romance, amusement, entertainment and adventure. And — he felt — only in the city could he enjoy the thrills of really living.

His dissatisfaction with the farm increased steadily — until finally he went to his father and said, "Dad, some day your wealth will be divided between my brother and me. You know how unhappy I am here. Please, won't you give me my share of the inheritance now?"

Again and again, he pleaded with his father — until, at last, the farmer yielded. The younger son was given his inheritance — and within days he was off to the city, off to the far country.

There he wasted his money. There he wasted his life — in what he thought was a wild and glorious experience. In reality, he sank deeper and deeper into a pit of depravity . . . corruption . . . wickedness . . . immorality . . . drunkenness . . . sin.

Finally, the bottom dropped out. A deep recession came into the life of the city. His money disappeared. His friends disappeared — for they were the kind of friends who could only be bought with money. His good times disappeared — tumbling round about him in a heap. He found himself alone . . . destitute . . . hungry.

No jobs were to be found — until, outside the city, he was hired by a farmer to feed the pigs. That's about as low as a Jewish boy could sink (remember how the Jews feel about pigs). There he was: out in the field, feeding pigs — and so hungry he was actually eating some of the garbage meant for the swine.

In the pigpen, he finally woke up ... came to his senses ... realized how stupid he had been ... determined to return to his father. "Back home," he said to himself, "my father has servants and workers who have plenty to eat — and here I am, starving. I've been a fool."

He made up his mind to go home ... confess his mistakes ... seek forgiveness ... and ask only to be a hired hand — not a son.

We remember what happened — it's such a familiar story. He did arise ... he did leave the pigpen ... and he did return home.

And there he was welcomed ... forgiven ... restored! His father was overjoyed! The boy was given a new robe for his body ... a new ring for his hand ... new shoes for his feet ... and the fatted calf for a feast! It was a happy time — a time for celebration, for music and dancing, for making merry!

Embarrass

This well-known tale illustrates how a life is turned around ... how a Christian life begins ... how a conversion to Christ often occurs. Three words describe this tremendous experience — and if we can wrap our own lives around these three words, it may be helpful.

The first of these words is Embarrass. The Prodigal Son, off in the far-away city, reached the point of embarrassment. He was not embarrassed when he left home. He was not embarrassed when he had plenty of money to fling around. He was not embarrassed when he thought he was enjoying a good time.

But it didn't turn out the way he had expected — sin never does! The far country — which seems so attractive and alluring from a distance — loses its sparkle and brilliance when it becomes the near country. Note the phrases from the Bible:

"a mighty famine" ..."he began to be in want" ... "into the fields to feed swine" ... "would fain have filled his belly with the husks" ... "I perish with hunger."

And finally the lad reached the low point of embarrassment. A sense of shame — and of guilt — swept over him. He became fully aware of how foolish he had been. He was depressed ... disgusted with himself ... and dwelt in the depths of despair.

There in the pigpen — a long way from his father's home — he "came to himself" (that's the way the Bible puts it). He recognized his failures; he admitted his mistakes; he confessed his sin.

And he thought out loud, "How foolish I've been. This is ridiculous — for me, the son of a rich man, to be here in a pigpen, suffering from hunger, willing to eat this garbage, when the servants back home have more than enough to eat. How stupid can I be?"

This is true in many lives. We go our own way. We take our lives into our own hands. We decide to satisfy our own selfish desires. Then ultimately, we reach the place where we become aware of our shortcomings ... of our separation from God ... of our sin and our stupidity.

Because sin degrades us, drags us down and destroys our self-respect. And to lose one's self-respect is devastating.

If we have no respect for someone else, we can stay away from that person. Even husbands and wives who have lost respect for each other can manage (if they wish) to put up a good front, continue to live in the same house, and go their own individual ways.

But you can never get away from yourself. You are the one person in the world with whom you must spend 24 hours a day. You cannot run from yourself — ever. And if you can't respect yourself, you're in poor company — all the time!

Oh, you may have some outward signs of success and popularity — you may live in an impressive house, possess a large bank account, work at a prestigious job, drive an expensive car. But deep inside, you must live with you and you know what you are really like.

The boy found himself in a pigpen — without friends, without food and without funds. He had reached the bottom. And then — he "came to himself." He saw himself as he really was. He was embarrassed — ashamed of his foolishness and stupidity (after all, that's what sin is). And in the moment that he "came to himself," his transformation, his renewal began.

So it is with us — we need to see ourselves as we really are. We need to take a long, frank, honest look at ourselves. What we see may not make us happy, or proud; it may embarrass us — but it is the first step toward redemption.

Embrace

The younger son — in a far country and in a pigpen — had made up his mind to go home. He prepared a speech. Then he arose ... left the hogs ... and started his homeward journey.

Before he arrived, his father — a long way down the road — was watching, and saw him approach. The Bible doesn't specifically say so, but the implication is that the father did this regularly — maybe every day. In any case, on that day, he saw a traveler coming toward him.

"Oh, my, that looks like him — it really does," he whispered. And down the road he went — running. The closer he got, the more certain he was — it really was his boy!

He ran quickly to the lad ... threw his arms around him ... and, tears streaming down his cheeks, gave him a warm embrace.

The son, with a lump in his throat, began the speech he had been rehearsing for days: "Father, I have sinned against heaven, and in thy sight, and am no more worthy to be called thy son . . ."

But the happy father interrupted ... ordered a robe and a ring and shoes for his son ... and commanded that the fatted calf be prepared for a time of feasting and celebration. "For," as the grateful father so eloquently explained, "This my son was dead, and is alive again; he was lost and is found!" The boy learned that day that his father loved him — really loved him."

And we need to discover the same truth — that God does love us, that he really loves us. This isn't just a trite platitude that we use — it's real ... it's vital ... it's true. God does love us. Like the father of the boy, God wants us back in his family, back in fellowship with him.

And when we reach the place of penitence ... of embarrassment ... of decision — God is more than ready to welcome us, to receive us into his outstretched arms of mercy, to draw us close to himself.

Yes, God is "more than ready" to embrace us. For the New Testament picture of our Christian God is not that of one waiting with open arms to receive us when we return to him. He is infinitely more. He doesn't merely wait — he takes the initiative ... goes out into the world ... enters into life itself, seeks and searches for that which is lost.

Jesus, in this parable, was not portraying the nature of God. Nor was he primarily concerned with the younger son. His main point was the older son. He was talking here to the scribes and Pharisees — and they were being compared with the older son. (And we haven't even mentioned him in this chapter until now!)

If it had been the purpose of Jesus to picture the essence of God in this story, he might have told this part of it a bit differently. Let us review.

The younger son received his inheritance ... went quickly to the far country ... recklessly squandered his substance ... reached the depths of despair ... and was feeding the pigs. Thus far, the story would be the same.

But as he sat on a stone in the pigpen, his head hanging low between his hands, the boy's thoughts went back home.

He realized he was a fool. He made up his mind. He was ready to arise and start home.

At that instant, he had a strange feeling — he just knew that somebody was there in the pigpen, with him. Haven't you sometimes felt that way — sensing that someone else was in the room with you, even before you saw them? So it was he — sensed a presence in the pigpen. As he heard a soft whisper, he quickly stood up and turned. And there he saw — his father!

"Why, dad, what are you doing here?"

"Son, I've been looking for you. I've hunted everywhere. I love you, son — more than you know. I couldn't stay home and wait. I had to see if I could find you. And now I have — I'm so glad."

And there, in the pigpen, they threw their arms around each other — and went back home — together.

That's the God who is pictured on the pages of the New Testament — not a God who stays at home and waits for repentant sinners to return, but a God who actually hunts . . . seeks . . . finds . . . and brings back . . . those who are lost.

That's the God of our Christian gospel: God in a far country . . . God in a pigpen . . . God in a gutter . . . God in a saloon . . . God in a sinful, foul-smelling hole of iniquity.

Yes, God is in every circumstance of life into which humans allow themselves to fall. We cannot flee from this seeking God.

Christianity proclaims a God who cares so much for his creatures — who loves them so deeply — that he cannot wait for them to come back to him. He must go out, he must hunt for them — amid their sin, their evil and their wickedness.

Christianity, you see, is different from other religions. They portray humans as seeking God — sometimes in strange, weird ways: by bathing in a dirty old river . . . by making a once-in-a-lifetime pilgrimage . . . by slashing and tormenting the human body . . . by offering a loved one as a human sacrifice.

But the New Testament teaches that God is seeking us. God is not lost — and we must find him. We are lost — and he must find us. We have wandered and gone astray — and he must hunt for us. He loves us that much. "The Son of man is come to seek and to save that which was lost (Luke 19:10)." He wants us — much more than we want him.

God really loves us — just as we are: with all our short-comings and failures and sins. "God commendeth his love toward us, in that, while we were yet sinners, Christ died for us (Romans 5:8)." Christ died for us — and that's how much God loves us.

He doesn't love what we do — but he does love us. That isn't hard to understand. Parents love their children. Often they misbehave or disobey. Yet the parents still love them — but not what they do.

Or look at yourself. You sometimes do things that you don't really approve of — but in spite of this, you still love yourself; you still think you're Number One.

So it is: God loves us — not what we do — but he does love us.

Embody

Now we must leave the son and his father — for our third word, Embody, describes something that God can do, but human beings just cannot do. He can actually get inside us — become one with us. Christian theologians call it "the indwelling of the Holy Spirit." The important thing, though, is not what we name it, but what happens.

I am sure that the father of the Prodigal Son wished that he could get inside his boy — now that he was back home — and live through him. But human beings can't do that. However, God is not human; he is divine ... he is Creator ... he is God. He is able to do what we cannot — he can get inside his creatures.

We try to do this with our friends and loved ones. When we receive word of an accident, a serious illness, a death, an unfortunate or tragic experience, what do we do? We want to be with them; we want to try to help; we go to visit them.

We arrive at their front door — and then wonder, "What on earth am I going to say?"

But it doesn't really matter — we don't have to say anything. We just need to be there — and be close to our friends.

Women have an advantage over men at a time like this. Men so often hold back their emotions — but women express theirs. What do they do? They throw their arms around each other, and hug. Words aren't important. They simply want to take some of the hurt ... carry part of it themselves ... share a bit of the sorrow.

And what we try to do — incompletely — God can really do. He can really get completely inside us. There is a little phrase in the New Testament which expresses this truth; it consists of just two words — "In Christ." Consider these passages from the scriptures: "If any man be *in Christ,* he is a new creature (2 Corinthians 5:17)." "There is therefore now no condemnation to them who are *in Christ Jesus* (Romans 8:1)." *"Christ in you,* the hope of glory (Colossians 1:27)." "Know ye not that ye are the temple of God, and that the *Spirit of God dwelleth in you* (1 Corinthians 3:16)?" "I am crucified with Christ; nevertheless I live; yet not I, but *Christ liveth in me* (Galatians 2:20)."

Here, in our union with our heavenly Father, we find the answer to life's deepest problem. Our deepest problem is not to find forgiveness. Other religions all provide some means of being forgiven for our mistakes and sins. What we ultimately need is not only forgiveness — but deliverance. Deliverance — so that we won't go back and do the same, stupid, sinful things all over again.

And God gives us this power, his power — by actually getting inside us and living in us ... through the inspiration and the indwelling of the Holy Spirit himself.

This is the key to Christian living. This is how God helps us overcome temptation ... defeat sin ... be victorious over evil. We are one with Christ — he literally gets inside us — and we "can do all things through Christ, who strengtheneth us (Philippians 4:13)."